# Grantham in the News
# 1926 - 1950

# Acknowledgements

Thanks to all the Journal reporters and photographers who recorded the town's activity during this quarter of a century together with local photographers including Walter Lee and Chris Windows. Also to Richard Adams and Tina Bishop for their help.

Thanks also to readers who allowed me to use their pictures, including: Elaine Lovegrove, Keith Harrison, Leilia Parker, G Ellwood, Ron Lee, Mike Matsell, Sue Redmile, Malcolm G Knapp, Pat Aveyard, Katherine Aspland, Gordon Baxter, Bill Davies, Christine Davies, Harold Ebb, Dave Fardell, Anne Mole, Stan Matthews, Hazel Tebb, Joan Parnham, Peter Beeby, Arthur McKown, Phyllis Nadin, Paddy Perry, Geoff Gardiner, Peter Nicholls, Brian Wright and Grantham Journal.

First published in 2009 by
John Pinchbeck
email: GranthamPast.@gmailcom
Website: GranthamPast.com

All rights reserved. No part of this book may be reproduced in any form or by any means, including information storage and retrieval systems without permission in writing from the publisher who may quote passages in a review.

Dedicated to my grandchildren, Abigail, Darcey, Evie and Kaelin, hoping they will never experience the war or want so many people featured in this book have.

Printed & Bound by Bell & Bain, Glasgow

ISBN: 978-1-902950-05-1

# Introduction

THIS was probably the most important 25 years in Grantham's history – the period which saw it go from bust to boom with an interruption by bombs.

It began with the General Strike and a depression and finished with workmen unable to find enough hours in a week to fulfill their companies' order books.

This is the era which saw the rebuilding following the First World War and the effects on the town as the world plunged into a second global conflict.

Yet life had to go on and the future to be planned. Crooks still robbed and pilfered and life had tragedies away from war.

It was the time when names such as Aveling Barford, BMARCo, Sullivans, Bjorlow, RH Neal and Newman moved in, providing thousands of jobs for skilled workers as the town entered a new age.

And when an errant eight-year-old could still be birched by police.

This book is as much to entertain and bring back a few memories than to bombard the reader with facts.

This is about real people, not just the 'upper crust' of the town and surrounding villages, but also the poor and the lawbreakers.

Throughout these pages there are lots of clues to the reality of life more than half a century ago.

Cash has been converted to modern currency for the generations who no longer understand the meaning of guineas, half-crowns or fifteen-and-six and many measurements are in metric for the same reason.

I hope you will enjoy reading it as much as I enjoyed researching it.

*John Pinchbeck*

**BMARCo's factory following a bombing raid in 1942**

# 1926 Grantham in the News

Business as usual at Ruston and Hornsby's foundry

## Town escapes worst of the General Strike

THE nine-day General Strike that brought the country to its knees had little effect on Grantham.

Although 900 of Ruston and Hornsby's workforce came out halfway through the eighth day, the 550 non-union members continued to work.

There were several meetings during the conflict but the biggest effect was the cheers as workmen learned it was all over.

High Street was choked with lorries and charabancs as the railway drew to a halt.

On the Sunday of the strike, 150 cars carrying strike-busting Oxbridge graduates to Hull dockyards, passed through town.

Daily bulletins were issued from the town Independent Labour Party's St Peter's Hill headquarters.

Additional special constables were sworn in to direct traffic.

The Theatre Royal, George Street, closed for two weeks due to the lack of transport for actors.

There was one casualty. RAF Cranwell officer Mr Stephenson, was on duty as a volunteer railway guard. He was hit on the head from behind with an iron bar wielded by a masked man in a brake van but recovered several days later.

## Boy dies in harvest tragedy

FARMER'S son Edward Seymour (11) died in a harvest accident at Top Farm, Billingborough.

The youngster had just completed his paper round when he arrived to help his father.

He drove the horse-drawn sail-reaper which was harvesting the wheat.

Meanwhile his father, Albert Seymour, fired his gun at a rabbit.

The horses were startled and broke into a gallop.

The youngster was thrown head first into the reaper's knives. He died before the doctor arrived.

Returning a verdict of accidental death, district coroner Dr Cragg said he was concerned that a boy so young should be employed on such dangerous work although waived his criticism as it was the farmer's son.

## Widow dies when grave stone falls

A 76-year-old Bottesford widow died after a new tombstone toppled on her.

Ellen Sharpe was in the village churchyard when she walked past the headstone which had only been put up the day before.

According to mason Arthur Challands, who saw the accident, she appeared to use it for support then collapsed.

The stone fell on top of her. She died two days later.

A spokesman for masons Streather and Winn, of Grantham, said the cement securing the gravestone had not dried.

## Miraculous escape for two airmen

GRANTHAM airmen had a miraculous escape when their aeroplane made a forced landing at Wykeham.

Flying Officer Gibb, and Aircraftman Hutchings, who were both based at Spitalgate Aerodrome, were flying the plane belonging to 89th Bombing Squadron, when it developed engine trouble.

As they attempted to land, the undercarriage struck an overgrown ditch, flipping the plane over.

The plane was a write-off but the two men managed to crawl from the wreckage with only bruising and scratches.

# Grantham in the News — 1926

## Mixed bathing at town lidos

THE council decided mixed bathing would be allowed at both of the town swimming pools.

Men and women were allowed to use Wyndham Park pool on Mondays and Houghton Road, soon to be renamed Dysart Park, on Thursdays between 6pm and 8pm

But calls for Sunday opening at Wyndham Park as well were rejected.

Coun Chalkley said it was hardly fair to other parts of town when Houghton Road would be.

He said: "It will drive people from one end of town to the other and Houghton Road will be inundated with swimmers.

The Mayor told him the only reason for the decision was under-use and the fact it would upset the cleaning programme.

## Welby Street to be one way

WELBY Street and Stanton Street became one-way – but only for buses.

Town councillors agreed to new traffic flows between Wharf Road and Wide Westgate, as buses could not pass each other.

A proposal for a complete one-way system for all traffic was thrown out as "too complicated".

Coun Rothwell Lee said he thought the whole scheme was unreasonable.

He said: "There is no undue congestion except when buses are passing.

"It would be ruinous for shopkeepers if vehicles could not go through the streets either way."

## Marriage off to a kick-start

FOLLOWING their wedding at St Wulfram's Church, Grantham, the happy couple set off on honeymoon by motorcycle. The bride rode on the pillion.

Her father said: "If the man thinks my daughter will always be contented with the back seat he is woefully mistaken."

## New club founded

THE Town and County Company was founded with £3,000 capital.

Formed as a social club, it was planning a swimming baths, bowling greens, skittle alleys and pleasure grounds in the town.

## Car repair shop open

JACKSON and Son was given planning permission to convert former maltings on the corner of Wharf Road and Westgate into a motor repair garage.

## Swimming coaches

THE borough council was advertising for both male and female swimming instructors to be employed at Houghton Road (Dysart Park) swimming pool at £3.75 per week.

## Traffic flow

A TRAFFIC survey on Springfield Road revealed 5,630 vehicles used the road in one week, a rate of about 80 per hour.

## Butchers coast it

BUTCHERS and their wives had their annual charabanc outing to Sandringham and Hunstanton, calling at Sutton Bridge for lunch.

## Oh boy!

COUNCILLORS were debating whether the new Boys Central School, which was being built on Sandon Road, should also be open to girls.

---

**Yarde & Co.** FINEST BLACK MALT AND KENT HOPS

For making 2½ Gallons HOME BREWED STOUT or PORTER

**CHEAPER BEER**

Brew your Own from our Noted Packets for making both

**ALE & STOUT**
1/- PER PACKET

Postage on one packet 6d.
Postage on two, three, or four packets 9d.

SOLD BY
**J. COX & SON**
CHEMISTS
36, Watergate, Grantham.

# 1926 Grantham in the News

## Boy dies in crow's nest plunge

A TEENAGER fell to his death while trying to reach a crow's nest. Daniel Avey (16), of Whatton, was walking with friends at Normanton, near Bottesford, when they spotted the nest 20m high in an ash tree.

He climbed the tree to see what was in it, but two-thirds of the way up he lost his grip and fell to the ground

One of his friends, Herbert Speed (15) called workmen in a nearby field but Daniel was pronounced dead at the scene by Dr Martin.

He died of a broken spine.

## Relief for parking chaos

TO relieve traffic congestion, the town council made an order authorising parking places on some of Grantham roads.

They were the south side of Wide Westgate (not Saturdays), Market Place (not Saturdays), and St Peter's Hill west of the green (Saturdays only).

Hackney carriages would be allowed to ply for hire on the east side of St Peter's Hill Green.

## Steel homes a success

TWO steel houses were built on Belton Lane by the town council, to demonstrate the amazing speed at which they could be erected.

Work began on January 6 and they were completed on February 25.

The three-bedroomed houses, near the destructor, cost £400 each to build which excluded land and drainage.

They were timber-framed with 2.5mm steel plate on the outside.

## Foot and mouth disease appears

THERE was an outbreak of foot and mouth disease at Waltham-on-the-Wolds.

It appeared at John Watson's farm in two or three pigs from a batch of 14 recently purchased.

A 15-mile embargo on movement was installed around the farm.

It came on the eve of what was expected to be Melton Cattle Market's biggest sale of the year.

## A cut above the rest

GRANTHAM woman Miss B Bruntlett stunned the crowd at the Roy Showground, Leicester, when she leapt from a plane with a parachute.

She left the plane at about 350m and went into freefall for the first 80m, doing somersaults as she fell.

She said afterwards: "It was very nice. Quite a sensation in fact."

## PC run over by milk float

PC Hallam was detained in hospital after the wheel of a milkfloat, pulled by a runaway horse, ran over his chest.

He was trying to grab the reins of the animal which had bolted from Read's dairy, North Street, when he was knocked down.

---

**NOT Coming
but
ALREADY ARRIVED**

THE IDEAL STORES,
IDEAL QUALITY,
IDEAL VALUE,
IDEAL SERVICE.

Why wait when the BEST is Here?
START to do your Shopping here NOW and be satisfied

Our Provisions
are the Finest Procurable, selected for their
Choice, Quality and Flavour.

We are Offering Splendid Value in
CHEESE, BACON, & HAMS.

**ROBERTS**
PROVISION MERCHANTS

1, 2, & 3, NORTH PARADE,
GRANTHAM

If more convenient for you, try our Branch at
Huntingtower Road.

**YOU WILL BE SATISFIED**

# Grantham in the News — 1926

## Unmarried mums double national rate

THE birth-rate in Grantham was the lowest ever.

The 335 births returned a rate of 1.74 per cent of the population. But of those, 27 were illegitimate - eight per cent - double the national rate.

Medical officer Dr C H D Robb said: "This must be considered a high figure and one to be regretted.

"The career of an illegitimate child is generally a very sad one."

There were 28 cases of infantile death, 11 of them due to congenital debility or premature birth.

Dr Robb said this was down by a third on what would have been expected before the Great War.

He said: "Improvements in living conditions and milk supply have gone a long way but the main reason is a psychological one.

"This is the realisation, amid the holocaust of war, of the true value of human life."

He said since the turn of the century, average life expectancy was 10 years longer than before.

During the past year Dr Robb reported there had been 39 cases of diphtheria, 69 of pneumonia and 53 of scarlet fever.

*The temporary library in 1925 which was replaced by a purpose-built building next to the Guildhall.*

## Readers get free library

GRANTHAM'S new purpose-built public library and museum was opened in May. In the first two days, 861 books were lent.

The building was on St Peter's Hill, near the Guildhall.

The first library in town - excluding the chained library in the parish church - was at the Philosophical Institution, Finkin Street, in 1840. It closed in 1858. There was a library in the Exchange Hall and later in the Guildhall, but these were not for general public use.

A free public library was first mooted in 1893 but a vote among the townsfolk established 460 in favour and 1,729 against. The need was rekindled in 1911 and this time the vote was won 1,562 votes to 960.

The war intervened before anything was done, but in 1922 it was finally established in temporary quarters. The cost of the new building was partly funded by the Carnegie UK Trust grant of £4,900.

## Labourer fell from hay wagon

FARMWORKER George Bryan, of Barrowby, lived for 66 days with a broken spine, before he died following a fall from a cart.

Dr Charles Frier told an inquest his condition had been hopeless from the start. Slow toxic poisoning set in and finally oedema of the lungs.

Mr Bryan, 37, a bachelor, was working at Barrowby Vale loading a hay wagon with a pitchfork from the top.

The horse moved forward and Mr Bryan slipped from the top of the cart. The coroner recorded accidental death.

## Birds fly home

MORE than 40,000 pigeons were released from Grantham in the Up North Combine young bird race.

Two special trains, one from South Shields, the other from Newcastle, arrived with a total of 50 wagons.

The birds were released from Ambergate yard sidings.

# 1926 Grantham in the News

## Youth ran away to sea

THE mystery of a Newton youth who disappeared without trace, was solved when he turned up in Rotterdam.

Harold Cecil Harbord failed to arrive at his job as clerk to the Clerk of the Grantham Board of Guardians one morning, having left home as usual.

In a letter to his parents, Harold said on impulse he decided to go to Hull where he stowed away on a boat.

After being caught, instead of handing him over the Dutch authorities, the captain offered him a career at sea.

## Farmer blames coal strike

LONG Bennington farmer Frank Mackley was fined 37p for allowing a cow and five calves to stray on to the public highway.

Sgt Needham said he examined the hedge containing the cattle and found there were two large gaps.

Pleading guilty, Mackley said people kept taking away parts of it for fuel during the miners' strike.

## New Seats

THREE new public benches were fitted on Dysart Road and another two on Harlaxton Road.

Alderman Golding also provided one for the corner of Wharf Road and Westgate.

## Boro is up for the cup after protest replay

BILLINGBOROUGH Football Club won the Culverthorpe Cup at the second attempt to round off a memorable season.

After beating Osbournby in the final at Oasby, there was a protest against L R Burgess, of Dowsby, who lived 180 metres outside the radius allowed by the rules of the competition.

In the replay, Billingborough won 4-1.

The club also made it a hat-trick of championships in the Bourne League.

## Chalked off

GEORGE Howitt of Sidney Street was fined 50p for having a motor vehicle with no index number conforming to regulations.

Sgt Wrag told Grantham Magistrates the number was chalked on the back of his lorry, which was not good enough.

## Meteoric rise

A FIREBALL was seen in the sky over Grantham, causing a stir as people left the pubs..

Shortly after 10pm on a Monday evening, the spectacle lit up the sky for several seconds.

Eye witnesses said it was a mixture of red, blue and green lights.

## Tremor rocks town

GRANTHAM residents were woken early when an earthquake rocked houses at about 5am one morning.

It lasted about two minutes. There were no reports of either injuries nor any damage.

## New cars on show at Ponton

NORTH Road Garages, founded in 1920, opened a new showroom at its Great Ponton workshop, by the side of the A1 trunk road.

While the dealership sold mainly Rover cars there was also a special display of the Chrysler Six.

**Staff at North Road Garages**

# Grantham in the News          1927

*Scholars meet on St Peter's Hill in homage to Sir Isaac Newton*

## Celebrations for bi-centenary

NEARLY 200 eminent academics from around the country gathered in Grantham to celebrate the 200th anniversary of Sir Isaac Newton's death.

The physicist and philosopher was born at Woolsthorpe by Colsterworth, was educated at King's School, Grantham, and buried in Westminster Abbey.

The celebrations were organised by the Yorkshire branch of the Mathematical Association with the co-operation of Mayor of Grantham Alderman Richard Brittain.

Among the celebrations was a visit to Woolsthorpe Manor and a rally in front of the great man's statue on St Peter's Hill, Grantham.

## Police pensions are far too high says councillor

A COUNCILLOR condemned police pensions as being a burden on the ratepayer.

His outburst came as the joint police superannuation fund committee was told it needed a further £3,000 to top it up.

They were told Sgt Talbot (46) had just retired after 25 years and was due to receive £175.95 a year pension.

But farmer Alderman Dean (75) said he received no pension and still had to pay tax at 57p in the pound.

He said: "There are men of 46, 50 and 52 in the prime of life getting £5 and £6 a week pension.

The people from whom the cash to pay them is being extracted in such a lavish manner should be given some consideration.

"It just isn't right."

Chief Constable James Casburn said he understood the alderman's concern and hoped one day there would be a more sensible policy.

## Costly trot for footpath riders

SARAH Cust, Lord and Lady Brownlow's daughter, was fined 50p at Spittlegate Court, for riding her horse on the footpath. When warned at Syston by Pc Thornton she claimed the road was not fit and there was no one on the path.

In a separate incident, George Morns, a groom, of Elsham Lodge, Grantham, was also fined 50p for riding on the footpath.

## Death traps removed at Foston

PLANS to upgrade the Great North Road were unveiled by the Ministry of Transport.

The trunk road between Gonerby Hill Foot and north of Long Bennington was to be brought up to scratch in a £100,000 major development.

More than 100 local men taken from the dole queue, would be employed on the project.

The road was widened to a minimum of six metres in the south and in Long Bennington, up to eight metres.

Kerbstones were installed along the route to strengthen the road and a 50cm drain put in.

The new road at Foston would by-pass the western part of the village, with a mile-long straight section from the Blue Boy Inn. This would remove the dangerous bends regarded as 'death traps'.

No properties were demolished in the Foston scheme.

9

# 1927 Grantham in the News

## Off key at the ball

THE key to the main door of Harlaxton Manor was stolen the night the Hospital Ball was held there.

The owner, Mr T S Pearson Gregory, said the Italian key was of no value to anyone but himself.

## New salon

ALICE Griffin, a ladies hairdresser at the Exchange Hall, High Street, for six years, moved to a new salon in the centre of High Street.

She took over from the Misses Dawson.

## Nasty slip up

ELIZABETH Smith (74) of Carlton Scroop, broke her leg and was taken to hospital after she had slipped on a banana skin which had been discarded in Westgate, Grantham.

## Silenced

THE eight bells of St Mary the Virgin Church, Bottesford, were taken down and re-hung on a new frame by specialists Taylors of Loughborough.

The total work cost of the work was £680.

## Traffic flows

A RECORD amount of motor traffic was logged on the main eastbond road from Grantham ro Donington.

At the busiest stage, the volume at Threekingham reached 300 vehicles per hour.

## Pigeon lays egg in bedroom

A PERSISTANT pigeon defied all efforts to ban her from a bedroom at a home in Billingborough.

She first flew in through the open window and built a nest on the dressing-table in the three-storey house in High Street.

The occupant cleared it away but the following day she found another nest complete with egg in the same place. The window was secured and bird was released several miles away.

But it took more than that to stop her.

She returned to the house next day, walked in through the front door and after visiting several rooms found her favourite dressing table and deposited another egg on it.

## Work starts on Earlesfield Hotel

WORK began on a new hotel following approval by town planners and licensing justices.

The Earlesfield Hotel, Dysart Road, was built by Mowbray's Brewery. The licence was approved after the owners closed down the Isaac Newton, Stanton Street, and Foresters Arms, Castlegate.

The building had a 30m frontage, all rooms facing the main road.

The entrance was placed centrally, with a central corridor for easy external police supervision.

A door on the east side allowed private access when a room is closed for a club or private function.

A spokesman said: "We are trying to provide a fully equipped modern hotel to serve the needs of a populous and growing district."

## Bolting carthorse leaps to its death

A HORSE delivering parcels to Kesteven and Grantham Girls' School, Sandon Road, died after it bolted.

The frightened animal, which belonger to carrier John Hall, careered along the road until it reached a wooden five-bar gate at the Hill Avenue junction.

But instead of stopping, the confused horse tried to leap over it.

Forgetting it was attached to a mail cart, it finished balanced across the gate on its stomach, with its forelegs on one side and hind legs on the other.

It was freed by builders working on the new Boys' Central School but it was in severe pain from the blow to its stomach..

The owner had it destroyed to prevent further suffering.

---

HOLIDAY OFFER     EUGENE     'PHONE 245

### Permanent Waving
at Greatly Reduced Prices for the Next Few Weeks.

FULL HEAD (SHINGLED)    £2 2 0
TOP & SIDES    £1 10 0
SIDE PIECES    15 0

Book Your Appointment Now. Personal Attention.
Consultation Costs Nothing. Call, Write or Phone

### Maison Sydney
(Ladies Hair Specialist).
PICTURE HOUSE, GRANTHAM.

# Grantham in the News    1927

## Shock killed crane driver

A GRANTHAM man was killed after falling from an overhead crane.

Charles Locke (51) a married man of Dudley Road, was working in Sheffield at the time.

A colleague said Mr Locke was on the platform of the crane and about to climb down the ladder. Mr Locke's face caught a live trolley cable which fed the crane.

He said: "I tried to grab him but I got a shock myself."

Mr Locke fell 12m to his death. The company's chief engineer told an inquest the trolley wires carried 500 volts.

He said the machine's guards had since been improved.

Mr Locke had worked for the company for only a week following a considerable period on the dole

## Cyclist hit PC trying to avoid an accident

ARTHUR Pullen of 3 Broad Street, Grantham, was fined 37½p after knocking over a policeman on High Street.

Pc Tomlin was on point duty outside the Angel and Royal Hotel when the incident occured.

The constable signalled for Market Place traffic to move, but then was felled by a heavy blow to his back.

A cyclist tumbled on him. The front wheel of the cycle was buckled by the force of the collision.

Pullen admitted negligently riding a bicycle.

He told Grantham Police Court he swerved to avoid two cars but instead skidded into the constable.

## Woman's bottom drawer pawned by rogue fiancé

A BRIDE-to-be was left in the lurch when her betrothed ran off with her bottom drawer.

Millicent Hyde, of Ilkeston, was due to marry Ernest Morley on July 30 but six days before the wedding he told her he had to return to Billingborough, where the couple were due to live.

He said it was to get the wedding certificate. He took with him two blankets, a counterpane and clothing worth £3.

A Nottingham pawnbroker told Ilkeston Magistrates, Morley had pawned the articles to buy a ring but later returned and pawned that as well.

Morley was jailed for three months for larceny.

## Dog raises cash for the sick

VENUS, the dog owned by Rose and Crown landlord Fred Gibson was a star when it came to raising cash for Grantham Hospital.

For wherever customers hide cash in the Swinegate pub - even deep in the dark cellar - Venus finds it and drops it into the collection box.

The wire-haired fox terrier filled one box with 70p and is well on the way to filling another.

Mr Gibson also charged 2p for each copy of the photograph (above), the proceeds of which were also donated to the hospital.

## Peer's son killed

THE Hon David William Ernest Duncombe, of Kirkdale Manor, Yorkshire died on the Great North Road near Colsterworth.

He was driving a small car which collided with a lorry.

He was thrown from the vehicle and sustained a fractured skull. He died shortly afterwards.

The lorry driver told an inquest the car was driving towards him in the middle of the road.

## Milk snatcher bound over

A 13-year-old boy was bound over for six months and ordered to see a probation officer each month after stealing a bottle of milk from a doorstep.

The youngster was delivering newspapers when he saw the milk and slipped it into his bag.

He told Grantham magistrates he was thirsty.

His father told the court he gave him a good thrashing and the boy had promised not to do anything of the kind again.

# 1927 Grantham in the News

## Beast swallows ball

BUTCHER J E Holland of Billingborough discovered a cricket ball inside a bull he was dressing. He said it must have consumed it while grazing. "It's amazing it didn't choke him," he said.

## School renamed

GRANTHAM Wesleyan School was transferred to the local education authority and renamed Wharf Road Council School.

## Stepping out

FOOTWEAR shops in Grantham closed for the day for the Grantham Boot Traders' Association annual outing.

They visited Cadbury's chocolate factory, at Bourneville, Birmingham.

## Jobless build road

UNEMPLOYED men were put to work building a road between Spittlegate and Cranwell aerodromes. The final stage, was the two-mile stretch from Cold Harbour to Londonthorpe.

The new road followed the former Roman road Ermine Street or High Dyke and was just less than 10 miles long.

## Dressed up

GROCER J E Stephens was among the prizes for window dressing at his two shops.

His displays promoting Shredded Wheat in his Commercial Road shop and The Savoy Stores, Wharf Road, both took top prizes.

## Och aye the snooze

A SCOTSMAN who nodded off on his journey from Dunfermline to Edinburgh was woken in Grantham.

The weary Caledonian slept for six hours on the train journey before Grantham staff, alerted by his wife in Edinburgh, awoke him.

She first contacted railway operator LNER at Doncaster.

As he waited for his train back to Scotland he dozed off again in the waiting room but managed to catch a later train. Whether he slept on the return journey was not recorded but if so he had an extra hour's kip.

As he travelled, the clocks were put back for the end of summer time.

The railway company said it was a genuine mistake and the man was not charged for the extra miles.

## Gramophone woman dies by roadside

ALICE Kidman (60) a widow of no fixed address, died on the roadside at Long Bennington.

With her son David (19) she travelled across the country pushing a pram containing a gramophone by which they made their living.

They had been playing their music at Grantham market on the fateful day and were walking to Newark, sleeping overnight in a barn.

Shortly after they had set off, the old woman collapsed.

Mr Kidman tried unsuccessfully to stop a car to fetch help.

Dr H B Jones, of Long Bennington, who attended her said she died of Bright's disease.

## Willing to serve

ARTHUR Nidd (24) was appointed verger of St Wulfram's Church, Grantham.

He had been a server for eight years and his father rang the bells for 28 years.

Before his appointment Mr Nidd worked at Ruston and Hornsby.

## Rail bridge rebuilt

NORTH Parade railway bridge was rebuilt to take heavier traffic.

The work used 90 tonnes of steel, 18 cubic metres of creosoted timber and 250 cubic metres of rock asphalt. The bridge was replaced in two halves on separate Sundays.

Two cranes, one 35 tonnes, the other 45 tonnes, were used to move the steelwork.

## Fatal blow

AN 11-year-old Swaton boy died after being kicked in the stomach by a mare.

George Burles did not complain of any pain until the following day.

He was taken to Grantham Hospital but an operation failed to save him.

---

**GRANTHAM SAVINGS BANK**
FINKIN STREET, GRANTHAM.
(Amalgamated with the York County Savings Bank)

With the sanction of the GOVERNMENT,
**COMPOUND INTEREST**
at the rate of

**£4**
PER CENT

is now allowed on deposits in the Special Investment Department, subject to three month's notice of withdrawal, calculated on monthly balances, without deducations or charges of any kind.

I. M HARDWICK
G. A. HARDWICK
Joint Local Actuaries.

August 1927

# Grantham in the News — 1927

## School becomes a hotel

DIANA Lodge, North Parade, was renamed the Hotel Diana.

It was bought by Mrs Talbot, of Nottingham, and turned into a residential and commercial hotel.

The hotel, next door to the King's School playing field, was originally a school.

It later became a hunting residence with stabling for French baker Monsieur Couturie.

There were 20 double bedrooms and a dining room for 30 people.

Two wirelesses were installed to entertain the guests.

## Coach comes off the rails

A RAILWAY coach derailed at a catch-point between Stoke tunnel and Corby, damaging the down line.

It was two miles before the driver realised what had happened and brought the train to a halt.

All trains had to travel on the up line the following day while repairs to the line were carried out.

## Hornsby men go for gold

GRANTHAM'S major employer, Ruston and Hornsby, presented gold medals and armchairs to employees with more than 50 years service with the company.

They were:

Henry Brown (66) of Chapel Yard, Barrowby, agricultural fitter with 50 years service.

William Henry Minkley (62) of Harrow Street, Grantham, an agricultural fitter for 51 years.

Robert Newcomb (63) of Brewery Hill, Grantham, an agricultural fitter for 51 years a similar period to William Robert Jackson (70) of Pond Street, Great Gonerby, an ovens fireman.

Joseph Lawrence (64) of Dudley Road, Grantham, a brush hand with 50 years service.

William Johnson (60) of Cecil Street, Grantham, a turner with 50 years service. He was only 10 years old when he started work.

## Parson in fracas

LITTLE Ponton clergyman the Rev Henry Pawson (26) was charged with assaulting John Phillip (27) a fruiterer, of Macclesfield Street, London.

There was a cross-charge of assault by the clergyman against Phillip.

Pawson appeared before London Magistrates with several facial scars.

It followed a fracas between the two men in a Chancery Lane flat although the reason for the dispute was not revealed to the court.

Both charges were withdrawn and Mr Phillip was ordered to pay the Rev Pawson's £1.05 doctor's bill.

*The new Dysart Park with impressive bandstand*

## Dysart Park opens formally

A LARGE gathering turned out at the former Houghton Road recreation ground as it was renamed Dysart Park.

Although it had been open to the public for some time, the official opening was deferred for the completion of the bandstand. A replica of the one on the Knavesmire, York, it could house a full-size military band.

The park was officially opened in July by the Mayor, Alderman Richard Brittain. The Earl of Dysart donated £100 towards the bandstand and a similar amount for building public toilets.

The park was described as a mix of areas to stroll and enjoy the flowers with plenty of recreation areas.

# 1928 Grantham in the News

## Too young to wed

AN application to grant permission for a 17-year-old boy to marry a 26-year-old woman was turned down by Grantham magistrates. They said he was not earning enough money to support her.

## On the airwaves

WIRELESSES proved popular in Grantham with 1,535 homes having licences issued at 50p each by the Post Office.

The hospital and workhouse also had sets for the inmates' entertainment.

## New bank opens

THE Midland Bank opened a branch in Queen Street, Bottesford. It was supervised by D D Stuart Carter the Grantham manager.

## A good show

RUSTON and Hornsby's standard binder, which won the silver medal at the Royal Agricultural Society show the previous year, took the gold award at the Royal Sussex Show.

## Speeding teacher

BARROWBY teacher Mabel Bird was fined 50p by Spittlegate Magistrates for riding a motorcycle without a licence.

Her boyfriend was on the pillion.

She said her licence had expired and in the excitement she had forgotten.

## Hero fails to save neighbour

A 24-year-old Grantham woman died when her clothes caught fire.

Dorothy Priest, of Manthorpe Road, was washing herself in the kitchen from a small bowl on a stool. Behind her was a pan of water on a gas ring.

Suddenly she called: "Help! My skirt is on fire!"

Her sister Jessie ran to her aid and tried to wrap towels around her. Jessie said her sister's muslin underskirt was alight.

She ran outside and called on neighbour William Goodwin for help.

He ran to the kitchen where he saw Dorothy sitting on a chair which also was on fire.

He brushed the blazing clothes from her and carried her outside.

Dr Parsons sent her to the hospital suffering from burns and shock.

Recording a verdict of accidental death at the inquest, coroner Aubrey Malim praised Mr Goodwin for his brave effort in trying to save Dorothy.

## Lost an eye

CONGREGATIONAL minister the Rev E B Mahan, lost an eye while watching a golf match in the New Forest.

He was hit with such force by a club, at one stage it was touch-and-go whether he would survive.

A doctor who was playing nearby stitched the minister's eye.

After his recovery he returned to his Castlegate church giving his sermon while wearing an eye-patch.

## Queer 'un says he'll quit town

THOMAS Featherstone, of Inner Street, known as Queer 'un because of his pet expression 'that's a queer'un', was fined £1 for trespassing in search of rabbits at Manthorpe.

He had 15 previous convictions, six of them for poaching.

Pleading guilty he told magistrates: "I have got a good job at Filey, in Yorkshire, driving donkeys on the beach this summer.

They are paying me £1 a week plus meals."

## Stop for tea and tee

A ROADSIDE cafe opened at Stoke Rochford called the Turn and Swerve.

Built on the side of the Great North Road next to the golf club, it had excellent views.

The timber building overlooked the greens and had a veranda for eating outside in all weathers.

The golf club charged £2.25 a year plus 7.5p per day green fees.

---

The PICTURE HOUSE GRANTHAM

TEL 245
NIGHTLY = at 6.30    SATURDAYS at 6.0
MONDAY, TUESDAY, WEDNESDAY,
THE GREAT EPIC OF THE GREAT WAR

THE SOMME

A NEW ERA PRODUCTION

# Grantham in the News 1928

## Bishop opens new school

THE contract to build the £3,527 Roman Catholic school, Sandon Road, was awarded to local builders Brown and Co.

The foundation stone for St Mary's School was laid by the Bishop of Nottingham.

The school was later opened by the Bishop of Nottingham and Bishop Pella.

It replaced the school that was on Barrowby Road.

**The Bishop of Nottingham lays the foundation stone**

## Flight record pair's disappearance over Atlantic Ocean is a mystery

MYSTERY surrounded the disappearance of a pilot and a society lady who went missing over the Atlantic Ocean.

Captain Raymond Hinchcliffe and the Hon Elsie Mackay, set off from Cranwell in their monoplane Endeavour hoping to become the first to fly the Atlantic from east to west non-stop. The feat had been achieved by airship but not by aeroplane.

The night before the fatal flight, they had a private showing at the Picture House of a film showing the Endeavour taking off and landing.

The couple planned the expedition in secret at the George Hotel, Grantham.

The night before the flight, Miss Mackay, the daughter of P & O shipping magnate Lord Inchscape, prepared enough sandwiches and vacuum flasks of soup and tea for three days.

On the fateful morning, the couple were driven by chauffeur from the hotel wearing their flying suits.

## Little girl killed by neighbour

A FOUR-year-old girl was killed after being hit by a car in Brook Street, at the end of Gladstone Terrace where she lived. Iris Fowler, had just crossed the road from the King's School and was stepping off the pavement to return.

She died of a fractured skull after being hit by an Austin 7 driven by a neighbour, Archibald Atkinson, who worked for the girl's father. Her mother said the girl was usually very wary of the road but sometimes hid from her in the King's School yard.

Dr F P N Parsons said the girl died from her injuries shortly after the accident.

Returning a verdict of accidental death, the jury cleared the driver of blame.

## Mansion demolished

COUNTRY mansion Syston Hall, near Belton, was demolished.

It was owned by demolition expert Thomas Lee.

Previously owned by the Thorold family, it was built in 1780 to replace the Old Hall, near Syston parish church, residence of the Hon Lady Thorold.

Sir John Thorold lived in a bungalow in the grounds and Syston Hall had been unoccupied since 1912.

The 50,000 bricks, 250-tonnes of stone and other materials were reclaimed.

Syston Park, was a popular venue for motorcycle racing and hill climbing events.

## Falling down

HEAVY traffic was blamed for a shop frontage leaning out dangerously.

Miss Lee's tobacconists of 22 High Street, was shored up and plates installed to stop it falling into the street.

# 1928 Grantham in the News

## No shop plea

A PETITION was handed to Grantham Town Council complaining about plans to build a shop on the corner of Sandon Road and Hill Avenue.

Householders on Hill Avenue said when they bought their new homes they did not expect them to be blighted by the wooden building.

## Refuse motorised

GRANTHAM Borough Council decided to buy motorised refuse freighters to replace the horse drawn ones.

They said it would save £433 a year.

Coun Clifford opposed buying them over seven years as he considered they would be scrapped after only four.

## Russian resolution

MRS G E M Chekanoff, manager of the Theatre Royal, George Street, Grantham, was granted a decree nisi against her Russian husband Nicholas because of his misconduct with a woman in London.

The couple married in 1916 when Mr Chekanoff was Inspector of Munitions for the Russian Government.

The case was not defended.

## Flying in

THE Air Ministry decided to give RAF Spittlegate a new name.

It became Grantham Aerodrome, home to the Flying Training School.

The new centre cost £200,000.

## No loos is good news

PLANS to put a shelter and public convenience on St Peter's Hill green, opposite the public library, were put on hold while borough councillors had a rethink.

Although they had approved the scheme a year previously, there had been a delay in starting the work.

Coun Alf Roberts said: "We must approach the whole question with an open mind."

He said he had visited the green on Whit Monday having been a supporter of the scheme, but now thought an alternative site would be better.

He said the scheme itself was imperitive to the town although he was confident the council could find a better place.

## Church closes

THE Wesleyan Church in Barrowby was closed after 95 years.

A later nonconformist chapel built next door by the Methodists continued to be open for worshippers.

## Youngest fryers

TOM and Kath Strickson outside Manthorpe Road fish and chip shop, on the corner of Prospect Place.

They were the youngest fryers in town.

It was run by their mother Jane Strickson.

## Paddy's progress

PADDY Myles, a greyhound owned by Ivy White, of Boothby Hall, Boothby Pagnell, won the Victoria Stakes at Long Eaton, his fifth win in nine races at the track.

---

SMART LOUIS HEEL 1-BAR SHOES,

in Patent
Black Glace
Brown Glace
Navy Blue Glace
from 21/- at

JEFFERY SMITH & SONS,
1, Watergate.

# Grantham in the News  1928

## Chicken brooder blamed for starting fire at hotel

A GRANTHAM hotel was burning while the telephone at the fire station went unanswered.

But firefighters still arrived in time to save a mother and daughter from the inferno.

The Red Lion, High Street, was badly damaged by the blaze which began at 2am one June morning.

Landlord John Keele was awoken by choking smoke. He woke his wife and the boot boy.

He rang the fire brigade and when he got no reply, he sent the boot boy, clad only in his nightshirt, to the police station.

Police arrived to find Mrs Wells and her three-year-old daughter at a top-floor window, trapped by the flames, preparing to jump.

They talked her out of leaping the eight metres until firemen arrived. Firemen Twilley and Andrew rescued them by ladder.

The £3,000 blaze was brought under control in an hour but not before the kitchen, bar and staircase had been gutted.

The cause was an oil chicken brooder in the kitchen. All but one of the 24 chicks perished.

## Shock death

TWO-year-old Monica Dodwell, of Charles Street, Grantham, died of shock after being scalded when her mother's arm was nudged as she poured out a cup of tea.

## Coaches overloaded

TWO Grantham bus drivers were each fined £2 by Bingham Court for overloading their coaches.

Charles Morris, of Wharf Road, Grantham, was stopped at Gamston, near Nottingham, with 26 passengers on his 14-seater coach.

William Howlett, of Laundry Cottages, Belton Lane, had 27 people in a similar vehicle.

## Black day for locos

RAILWAY company LNER repainted all 340 express locomotives black instead of the familiar green.

A spokesman for the company said the new colour made it cheaper to clean and maintain them.

The red lining on goods locomotives was also abolished.

## Whalebone is damaged by weather

THE whalebone arch, which spanned Whalebone Lane between Somerby Hill and Little Ponton, was broken by two trees which blew down in a gale.

It was believed to have been brought from Grimsby by seafarer William Daye, who lived at Little Ponton Hall, and died in 1741.

It was said he had installed three such arches in the grounds of his home.

## Obstructive rector

BITCHFIELD rector, the Rev C M B Skene, was fined £1 for causing an obstruction in Finkin Street.

He had parked his car a metre from the pavement while he went shopping.

He told Grantham police court he took longer than planned.

Sergeant Leeson said the car blocked the street for more than an hour and no one could get past.

Mr Skene said: "I can leave my car anywhere I like in London without any fuss at all.

"What's wrong with Grantham?"

## Rector weds

THE Rev Edwin 'Monkey' Millard, Rector of St Anne's Church, was married in Wandsworth.

His bride was Phyllis Sherrington Robinson.

**The whalebone before the mishap**

17

# 1928 Grantham in the News

## Toddler died after falling into tin of boiling dripping

A TODDLER died after falling into a dripping tin her mother had just taken from the oven.

Cyril John Johnson was in the tiny kitchen of his Broad Street home, when his mother took the tin out of the oven.

She put it on the floor and went to get some paper to put on the table.

Fourteen-month-old Cyril, meanwhile, was climbing on a box to reach the table. He slipped and fell into the meat tin containing boiling fat.

Mrs Johnson said it was the first time she had left the hot tin on the floor.

Dr Charles Cameron told an inquest he went to the child's home and found him suffering from a septic scalp. He said he died three days later from septic absorption caused by the scald.

Nurse Sheehan, of the Victoria Nursing Home, who attended the child, said the scald was extensive, from the crown of his head down to the back of his neck.

Recording accidental death, coroner Aubrey Malim said: "It was an accident that could have happened to any child, especially in a tiny room."

## Hospital cleans up with bigger laundry

GRANTHAM Hospital laundry was updated after more than half a century.

It was enlarged by using the former mortuary and a wooden hut erected for sorting out the washing.

Hot and cold water was provided to supply coppers and boilers.

A power mangle was also introduced and a drying chamber used five-metre drying horses, each with seven rails.

Heat for the flat irons came from a new stove.

The cost of the new laundry, including the introduction of electricity, was £886.

## Brothers in chores put in many years at Hornsby

THREE Grantham brothers celebrated 162 years service with the same company.

They were all fitters at Ruston and Hornsby.

Holmes Woodcock of 13 Stuart Street, completed 56 years, George, of 20 Stuart Street, 54 years and Arthur, of 12 Victoria Street, 52 years.

Holmes had retired in June but the other two brothers were still working.

Their father, Robinson Woodcock, was a blacksmith at Richard Hornsby for 20 years, who died in 1871 aged 47.

The trio were born in Spring Gardens, off London Road, opposite the firm's foundry.

They were jointly presented with long service medals.

## Meccano boys' club building up

A GRANTHAM branch of the Meccano Club was opened in spring, meeting every Friday, at the Earlesfield church hut.

It was for boys aged 8-14 which the club helped turn into young engineers.

The club soon had 62 members, and also ran two soccer teams, a cricket team and a gymnastics section.

*Councillor Sharpe (seated centre left) and his team*

## Sharpe shooting on the green

A FRIENDLY bowls match was arranged to open the bowling green in Wyndham Park.

It was organised by Coun William E Sharpe between two representative sides. The result was 58pts each.

# Grantham in the News 1929

## Outcry as eight-year-old gets birching

THOUSANDS of Grantham trade unionists sent a protest to the Home Office following the birching of an eight-year-old boy.

The National Association of Railwaymen and the 60-strong Grantham branch of the Railway Women's Guild called on the Home Secretary to condemn the sentence by Grantham Magistrates.

Petitions were also sent to the Lord Chancellor and the Clerk to the Justices telling them of their grave concern.

They were dismayed when the Home Secretary refused to intervene.

The youngster had stolen a £1 note and two gold wrist watches worth £4.85, belonging to Annie Allen, of Harlaxton Road.

He was sentenced to a year's probation together with six strokes of the rod.

His mother Maud, of Alexandra Road, was also fined £2 for receiving.

The youngster had been playing with Mrs Allen's nine-year-old son at their home.

The property was found to be missing shortly afterwards and Mrs Allen called police.

After first denying the theft, the boy then admitted spending the stolen money on cigarettes and chocolate.

## Claypole magnate dies at top hotel

ONE of the world's richest men died at the Ritz Hotel, London.

The story of Claypole-born Harry Coulby was a true rags-to-riches tale.

The son of a farm labourer, he left school at 14 and worked in a signal box at Newark.

After moving around with LMS railway comnpany, he sailed to the West Indies, working on the submarine telegraph.

Following a spell in Durban, South Africa, he travelled to New York in the USA.

He tramped hundreds of miles across America, sleeping under the stars and eating turnips.

His luck changed when he got work as a shipping clerk at Pittsburg Steamship Company.

He worked his way up until he became its president.

He never forgot his roots, spending hundreds of pounds to improve the village church. He also built the village hall in 1923, one of the finest in the country.

He was buried in the village of his birth and the village hall was closed for a week as a sign of respect to its benefactor.

**Knipton Brass Band entertain the crowds from pump manufacturers A C Potter's lorry**

## Twenty vehicles join big parade

MORE than 20 motorised and horse-drawn decorated vehicles paraded through the town in September, as part of the annual rag to raise funds for Grantham Hospital and National Children's Homes.

The Mayor of Grantham was 'arrested' and ransomed for £20.

Festivities began at noon when a party of Victorian ladies greeted the Sudbrook Riviera Express at Grantham station to welcome Camaralzaman, uncrowned king of the Orient, who led the parade on horseback.

Pirates paddled along the River Witham in the Jolly Roger to Wyndham Park where the parade started.

It went from Hill Avenue to Sandon Road, down Avenue Road (including what was later called Stonebridge Road) and along High Street.

# 1929 Grantham in the News

## Tailor sells up

GENTLEMAN'S outfitter Tryner Lynn sold his 70 High Street business to Mr H H Cox.

Mr Cox had managed the business for the previous 26 years.

Ex-Mayor Mr Lynn had been in business for 44 years.

## Grand hall

ALLINGTON village hall, a gift from Sir George Welby and Lady Dallas, was officially opened. The brick-built hall had a wooden block floor, ideal for dancing.

It was opened by the Bishop of Lincoln, Dr Swayne.

## Corn man bust

CORN merchant Joseph Bee of Corner Croft, New Beacon Road, went bust with debts of £493 and no assets.

The previous year he had shown a £15,000 loss.

He blamed "Bad trade and living beyond my means".

## New bus depot

LINCOLNSHIRE Road Car unveiled plans for a bus depot and garage on Huntingtower Road.

The contract for the brick building was awarded to A E Brown and Co of Grantham.

## New traffic lights

AN experimental traffic light scheme was installed outside the Angel and Royal Hotel at a cost of £125.

It was paid for by releasing a police constable from traffic duties there.

## Baptist Church rebuild starts

WORK to replace the Baptist Church began in June.

It was built on the Wharf Road site of the chapel, which had been pulled down six years previously after being condemned as unsafe.

Work by Read and Davey cost £3,600.

After laying of foundation stones, a service followed in the Congregational Church, Castlegate.

## Engine topples

A TRACTION engine overturned after the road beneath it collapsed.

The engine, which was towing a caravan and water bowser, crashed through a hedge and down a four-metre bank at Owthorpe, near Bingham.

Driver William Charman, of Norton Street, Grantham, was seriously injured and transferred to Newark Hospital.

## Passengers escape from burning bus

PASSENGERS travelling up Somerby Hill in Joe Bland's bus, beat a hasty retreat when it caught fire.

The driver had pulled in for petrol, some of which splashed on to the hot exhaust pipe. Passengers escaped through the emergency door before the bus was engulfed.

Firefighters from Grantham Aerodrome were first on the scene, but the bus was gutted.

## Whistful Wolves

THREE hundred players took part in a Christmas whist drive at the Westgate Hall in aid of Thursday Wolves Football Club.

---

**BUY LOCAL MANUFACTURED GOODS**

**BELL'S Self-Raising Flour,**

Unequalled for Cakes, Pastry, etc.
SOLD BY GROCERS AND BAKERS EVERYWHERE.

or apply to sole manufacturers

**LETTS' XL DEPT., ROLLERMILL**
GRANTHAM

AGENTS WANTED          BEST POSSIBLE TERMS

# Grantham in the News    1929

## Excluded child must go to school

AN inspector blamed Inner Street living conditions for a woman not sending her daughter to school.

He said eight-year-old Rose had been turned away from Huntingtower School because she was flea-infested. School attendance officer Robert Collect said the girl missed school as she was excluded on the advice of the medical officer for being in a 'verminous condition'.

He told magistrates the mother-of-six had been instructed on how to clean the child but had failed to do so.

He said: "In fairness the conditions in which she lived were bad – the house is condemned – and it was hard to keep the children clean."

The mother was fined 20p.

## Huge hitting Bader is too much

GRANTHAM cricketers came unstuck when they played against Cranwell cadets.

Neither opener scored and the team was dismissed for 50.

Big-hitter Douglas Bader, who became an ace fighter pilot in the Second World War, starred for the RAF team with an unbeaten 99. This was despite fine Grantham bowling from Tipping and Walsh.

Bader was one of only two Cranwell batsmen to hit double figures.

## Poor treat

TWENTY women from the workhouse were given a special treat by the lady assistants at Waterloo House, High Street.

They provided the ham and fish sandwiches, swiss rolls, cakes and pastries for the trip around Belvoir, Frog's Hollow, Marston and Westborough.

The transport was provided free by bus proprietor Joe Bland who also gave each inmate a stick of rock.

## Airship misses the town

HUNDREDS of golfers at Belton Park had an excellent view of airship R101 which flew four miles to the east of Grantham.

It was travelling towards Lincoln. It was on a 1,000 mile, 30 hour endurance flight which began and ended at Cardington airport.

## Father fined for being drunk in charge of child

A LABOURER from Union Court, Inner Street, Grantham, was fined 50p for being drunk in charge of a child under three years old.

He was holding his daughter's hand on St Peter's Hill, when stopped by police.

He told them had taken her to the Empire Theatre, George Street, and they were on their way home.

He admitted he had drunk too much at the football match during the afternoon.

He promised to take more care of his young family in future.

**Local girl Muriel with the tank for sale**

## Tank loses battle for survival

A TANK which had been presented to the town after the end of the First World War, was sold for scrap.

Grantham Town Council agreed to accept £26.50 for it.

It had first stood on St Peter's Hill Green, before being transferred to Wyndham Park, in keeping with the park's status as a war memorial, its most recent resting place.

# 1929 Grantham in the News

## Town gets new police station

WORK began on a new police station, behind the Public Library, on St Peter's Hill.

It replaced the meagre premises the force had endured for too long.

The Chief Constable had occupied a small office at the front of the Guildhall, while a small room behind had to serve all other duties. The cells were not adequate.

The mortuary had already been pulled down - about 50 years after it should have been replaced.

The premises had been condemned several times by a Home Office inspector.

The new station, single storey, with a modern flat roof, included a Chief Constable's Office, charge room, waiting room, sergeants' room, three male cells and a female cell.

There was also an exercise yard for prisoners.

## Island of wood for junction

A TRAFFIC island to help pedestrians cross the busy road was installed in St Peter's Hill junction with London Road.

It was placed in the centre of the area where five roads converge.

The island was made of timber to easily be removed if it didn't work.

## Airport plan off to a flier

FOLLOWING talks with the Air Ministry, the town council development committee agree to build an airport just outside of town.

According to an Air Ministry spokesman, every town of any importance would have a civil aerodrome, just as it has a railway station and roads.

He said although RAF Grantham was available to civil aircraft for refuelling and emergencies, there were no facilities for passengers or transferring freight.

The site was dependent on the cost of land but it was hoped the former Harlaxton airfield, Gorse Lane, would be available.

SOME BUY A BETTER CAR.

OTHERS BUY THE BETTER PETROL

Pratts

Every Car is a Better Car on Pratts

## Big hitters from Gonerby

GONERBY School Cricket Team - winners of the Journal Cricket Trophy. From left, back - Lloyd Cunnington, Roy Pulfrey, Tom Durrands, Bill Munton, Sydney Goss & Arthur Gibson; middle - Dick Summerfield, Harry Gibson, Frank Dodd, Robin Sentance, and Gordon Calbert; front - Willy Green & Arthur Sneesby

# Grantham in the News — 1929

## Gasworks boss pocketed cash

THE manager of Grantham Gas Works was fined £10 after pocketing £25 of company cash.

The cash was paid by scrap dealer Charles Spick, of Union Street, for surplus metal.

But Ernest Shadbolt was cleared of conspiracy to defraud his company of £97.75 in conjunction with John and Charles Barker, of Westgate.

It was claimed the Barker brothers invoiced the gas works for products it never supplied.

Grantham Magistrates ruled there was a lack of evidence to convict the brothers.

Shadbolt, the son of Robert Shadbolt, the previous manager, had been employed at the gas works for more than 20 years.

He was sacked from his £450 per year job, which had included a house and free coal.

## No ifs nor butts

HOUSEHOLDERS on the Hooley estate, Dysart Road, would not be given free water butts, despite a directive by central Government.

The Ministry of Health told the town council to install 90 water butts, but the local authority said "It was not found possible."

## Town gridlocked

GRANTHAM was gridlocked when a rear wheel came off a heavily laden lorry on High Street, between Guildhall Street and Finkin Street.

Fortunately the wheel stopped before it collided with an oncoming car. It was three hours before the wheel was replaced and the lorry continued its journey.

## Well! What a rum find

A TEN metre deep well was discovered by workmen making structural alterations at the Red Lion Hotel, High Street.

The well, a metre in diameter, was lined with carved stones up to 30cm thick.

Archaeologist Henry Preston said: "It may possibly be Roman workmanship. It is an unusual piece of work, the inside being beautifully carved."

*Some members of the Springfield parade*

## Plea to support new playing field

CHILDREN and their parents held a fancy dress parade at Springfield playing field.

Starting outside Springfield Mission, the parade marched up Victoria Street, down Stamford Street, along to Huntingtower Road, Harlaxton Road and Alexander Road before returning.

They collected cash along the way.

They were raising funds to equip the playing field in view of the danger posed to children by the increased traffic on Springfield Road.

## Priest in court over noisy service

THE Rev Wilfrid Francis was furious at a demonstration against his appointment as priest-in-charge at Boothby Pagnell.

He took John Todd, of Northallerton, Yorkshire, before Spittlegate Magistrates for unlawfully disturbing him while celebrating divine service.

Mr Todd, patron of the Boothby living, said his protest was at Mr Francis' appointment.

He said Francis was not his first choice and was angry that his views at the appointment were not taken into account by the parochial church council.

# 1929 Grantham in the News

## Sweet retirement

MR and Mrs Cave retired as caretakers at Kesteven and Grantham Girls' School after 16 years. They were presented with a cheque by head girl Bessie Ledger.

The Caves opened a sweet shop on the corner of Castlegate and Redcross Street.

## Cable sparks trouble

AN electric cable which sparked under a gas pipe caused a fire at the High Street home of chemist John Newcombe.

The subsequent explosion blew plaster off the walls.

## Boxes for police

POLICE boxes costing £44 each were installed at the western ends of Springfield Road and Barrowby Road.

Each contained a desk, telephone, ambulance box and a flashing blue lamp.

## High fliers

LADY Maud Hoare DBE laid the foundation stone of RAF College, Cranwell.

Previously, tuition had been provided in wartime huts.

## Forgetful priest

THE Rev Philip Evans pleaded guilty to having no lights on his motor vehicle at Foston.

The Vicar of Long Bennington told Spittlegate Magistrates he forgot to switch them on after dropping off at the institute to offer prayers after choir practice.

He was fined 25p.

*The granary being demolished*

## Wharf granary demolished

THE granary at the Old Wharf was demolished.

Over the years it had also been used as a general store and a house for pleasure boats.

During the Great War it was an ammunition store for troops stationed at Belton Camp.

## Cheery Joe doubles his fine

BUS owner Joseph Bland was fined £2 for acting as a conductor without a licence and his driver Walter Mears (24) £1 for also having no licence.

Bland (38) told Leicester Police Court: "Take another £3 for your infirmary."

Magistrates thanked him but urged him to obey the law.

## Lucky escape

A PILOT from the flying school, Grantham Aerodrome, had a lucky escape when his plane nose-dived over Old Somerby.

He parachuted to safety as the plane buried itself up to its wings in a field owned by farmer George A Jenkinson.

## Victor victorious

SIR Victor Warrender was returned as MP for the Grantham division.

He polled 16,121 votes, a majority of 4,098 over Liberal R H Brown.

Labour's M W Moore was third with 11,340 votes.

Nationally, Labour overturned a 183-seat Tory majority.

# Grantham in the News      1930

## Bus overturns at Foston Beck

SEVEN people were injured when a coach travelling from London to Newcastle overturned at Foston.

The all-night service swerved to the side of the road at Foston Beck on the Great North Road. A tyre-burst was blamed.

The 20 passengers were thrown from their seats.

Villagers and passing motorists helped in the rescue and administered first aid.

Seven people were treated for shock and bruising at Grantham Hospital.

The driver was unhurt.

## All disquiet on the library front

THERE was outcry among readers when they were told Grantham Public Library had banned a top-selling book.

Three separate petitions were raised protesting at the town council library committee's refusal to stock E M Remarque's All Quiet on the Western Front.

Councillors said it was "unsuitable" for the town's readers as it observed the Great War from the German side.

One disappointed reader said: "It is not about glory, it tells the horrors of the conflict."

Councillors were unmoved and refused to change their minds.

## Buttoned up

BRITISH Corosit Button Co moved from Homerton to Grantham.

It took over the former canalside Shaw's tannery works, off Harlaxton Road.

## New low cost housing scheme completed

THE Turnor Crescent housing scheme of 64 non-parlour houses was completed.

The site was described as "Midway up the Harrowby Hills".

It commanded magnificent views of the Witham Valley and the wooded country on the outskirts of the town.

It was named after Mayor of Grantham Christopher H Turnor in recognition of his services to the scheme.

The average cost per house, including sewers, was £279.

The land was bought from Colonel de Paravicini, of St Vincent's, for 2.5p per square metre, who also donated half a hectare of land.

The total cost per house including road works was £319.

The main qualification of tenancy was a limit of £2 per week income.

Priority was given to slum dwellers, people in lodgings and war pensioners.

Mr Turnor guaranteed a £5 per year prize to encourage cultivation, for the best gardens which would be judged by professional gardeners.

Rents, including rates, were set at 22.5p per week for three bedroom houses and 51.5p for the five bedrooms.

## Steel sleepers for railway

RAIL operator LNER began a programme of replacing its wooden sleepers with steel ones.

The first replacements were between Allington junction and Sedgebrook on the Grantham-Nottingham line

The company ordered 1,500 tonnes of sleepers, approximately 15,800 of them.

The main advantage of steel sleepers was being manufactured in the UK while timber ones had to be imported.

A spokesman said it would change the tradional sound of railways.

# 1930 Grantham in the News

## Line for emergency

A TOWN councillor said Grantham Hospital should be provided with a telephone.

Ald Rowe said: "It is vital in case of serious illness or fire."

## Hands down

THE town council gave £600 towards the £900 cost of converting a dozen cottages in Hand's Yard into six. The rent was fixed at 18p per week.

## More parking space

GRANTHAM Town Council bought 1,200sq m of land on the corner of Welham Street and St Catherine's Road, for parking cars and buses.

## Hospital closure

THE Ministry of Pensions Hospital, Harrowby Camp, closed. Patients were transferred to Orpington.

The hospital, opened in May 1921, was set in countryside surrounded by gardens. Patients had cricket and bowls teams.

## Two die in air crash

PILOT Flt Lt James Bloomfield, of Southampton, and Ac Cyril Williams, of Northwich, died when their plane plunged 300m and crashed at Grantham Aerodrome.

## Farm sale

THE 100-hectare Fulbeck Low Fields Farm with a farmhouse, two cottages and outbuildings was sold for £2,400.

## Lightning strikes former workhouse

LIGHTNING struck the County Institution on Dysart Road, ripping 80 tiles from the roof.

Another strike destroyed the roof of a new house on Walton Gardens.

Although lasting only a few hours, the storm caused considerable damage to property.

Hailstones, some larger than golf balls, fell making the pavements treacherous and dangerous for anyone to venture out.

Lightning also struck the chimney of Mr Cottam's house in Carlton Scroop, which crashed through the roof.

It also caused the property's washhouse to catch fire.

The 200-year-old disused windmill at Foston, owned by Mr Rowbothom, was struck for a second time splintering much of its timbers.

## Five years for schoolgirl thief

A TWELVE-year-old girl was sent to a reformatory school for five years and her mother fined £2 by Grantham Magistrates.

The girl admitted she had stolen a quantity of material, including towelling, silk and lace, worth £3 from the National School, Castlegate.

Her mother, of Grantley Street, was charged with receiving the goods

She pleaded not guilty.

The headmistress said she discovered the goods were missing and went to the girl's house.

She saw some of the missing goods on a sofa.

The woman claimed her daughter said she had been given them by a teacher and returned everything.

Magistrates said the woman deserved more than a fine but that would be unfair to her other children.

**The airship at Little Ponton**

## Airship lands at Little Ponton

AN airship which had set off from Cramlington, Northumberland, stopped at Little Ponton to refuel.

Owned by the Airship Development Company, it was on its way to Folkestone, from where it was to be used for advertising purposes over London.

It landed in Mr Todd's field near Little Ponton Hall.

It stayed longer than planned due to a 40mph headwind.

This was good news for local bus companies who quickly organised trips to see the airship.

## Land set aside for Grantham airport?

LAND on the south side of Dysart Road, between Earlesfield and Barrowby, was earmarked as the site of Grantham's civil airport.

About 70 hectares of land was approved by the Air Ministry following an inspection by officials.

A borough council spokesman refused to confirm the plans.

He said: "The land has been licensed by the ministry but we are at the talking stage.

"It's all a bit in the air at the moment."

# Grantham in the News     1930

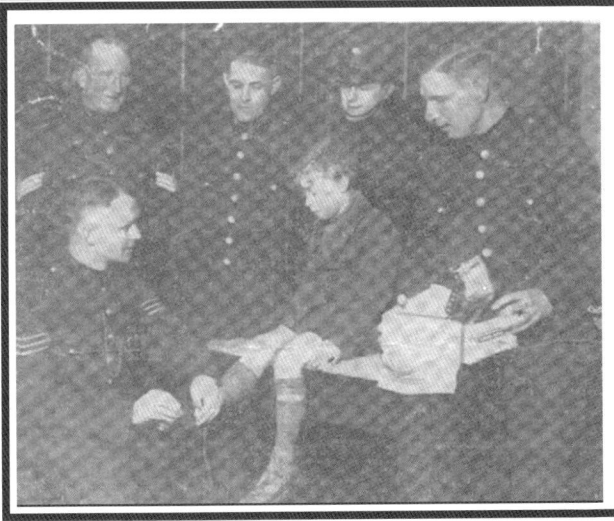

## Public tight on coppers

A SILVER collection at a concert for the Grantham Police Boot Fund raised a mere £6.65 - even though more than 700 people turned up.

More than £1 was in copper coins, much of it in halfpennies.

The excellent concert at the Theatre Royal, George Street, was well received but the tight-fisted audience failed to put their hands into their pockets.

The fund provided footwear for the town's poor children.

**Left: Police present a youngster with a pair of sandals**

## Three-year sentence for fourteen-year-old boy

A 14-year-old boy was sent to a reformatory school for three years for stealing 10p.

He was given the money by market stallholder Miss Ray Mark of Nottingham to buy butter.

But when he failed to return from the errand, she called police.

Miss Mark said the youngster had run errands for her in the past without any problems.

Pc Bell said the boy admitted the theft and immediately returned 7p.

The youngster said he was hungry and spent the money on sweets, fish and potatoes.

Grantham Magistrates were told there was no parental control at home and he was absent from school 31 times out of a possible 162 attendances. Last time he had seen his mother he was abusive and insulting.

## Pilgrims progress

NEARLY 500 pilgrims turned out at Birthorpe, near Billingborough. They arrived by road and rail from all over Britain.

Members of the Christian Convention for the Deepening of Spiritual Life, planned to meet yearly at Birthorpe.

There were public baptisms for new converts as preachers said they hoped to be a major religious force by the end of the millennium.

The pilgrims had a few hours rest at sunset before returning to their devotions in the early morning.

## Bakery blaze

A BAKERY owned by Henry Bell was destroyed by fire.

The two-storey Westgate building, next door to Currys, was gutted and the machinery inside was beyond salvage.

The cause of the £900 blaze remained a mystery.

---

**Play with DUNLOP TENNIS RACKETS**

DUNLOP DE LUXE Price 75/-
DUNLOP NATURAL GUT Price 72/6
DUNLOP POPULAR Price 55/-

DUNLOP TENNIS BALLS Price 14/6 PER DOZ

DUNLOP RACKET PRESSES
IN WOOD 4/6    ALL METAL 8/6

TENNIS RACKETS in Stock by "AYRES" "SLAZENGERS", "WISDEN", Etc
From 12/6 to 72/6
We also carry a Large Range of all SUMMER SPORTS GEAR
SPECIAL TERMS FOR CLUBS
RE-STRINGING AND REPAIRING RACKETS OUR SPECIALITY.

**HENRY COLLARD**
THE SPORTS SHOP, WATERGATE, GRANTHAM

# 1930 Grantham in the News

## Fuselage ride of terror for Spittlegate hero

SPITTLEGATE School old boy George Wilson, an engineer with Imperial Airways based at Jask, Iran, had the flight of his life after rescuing a woman in the desert.

He was called out after aviator, the Hon Mrs Victor Bruce, crash-landed in the desert while flying solo in her tiny aircraft from Bushite in the Persian Gulf.

She was found by tribesmen who sent for help.

Mr Wilson, of Albert Street, Grantham, arrived and repaired the machine but had no means of getting back.

Mrs Bruce offered him a lift back for the 200 mile journey but there was no spare seat.

Instead he spent the journey clutching the fuselage.

Afterwards Mr Wilson (26) said: "My heart was in my mouth. It was the longest day I have lived."

After leaving school at 13, Mr Wilson joined Ruston and Hornsby's before going into the RAF. He had worked at Jask for about a year.

## Dirty trick by police claims bus driver

BUS-owner Joseph Bland criticised Leicester Police for tricking him into breaking the law.

Mr Bland, who had been previously fined by the Ministry of Transport several times for breaches, said he was indignant and angry at his latest appearance before them.

He said a plain-clothes officer got on to his bus at Leicester Haymarket requestintg a ticket for Grantham.

Mr Bland told himhe must go to the tram terminus as he did not have a return ticket.

Mr Bland said: "He pleaded with me several times and I finally felt sorry for him and took him.

"When we got to Grantham he said 'now I'm going to break your heart'.

"Such tactics are a disgrace to the force."

## Died after engine test

A YOUNG man died of his injuries when a flywheel burst at his workplace.

Edward Standen (19), of Dudley Road, was testing an oil engine when the accident happened.

He was taken to hospital where the metal was removed,

Dr Frier said the youth had a fractured leg beneath the knee, flesh wounds either side and knee wounds. He died of septicaemia.

The cause of the wheel-burst was a mystery.

## Charles was worthy of notes

CHARLES Freeman, of Victoria Street, asked magistrates to make the police hand over two 10-shilling notes (50p) he had lost in the Market Place.

He said they had been handed in at the police station the same day, but officers refused to give him them back.

Magistrates agreed to wait until the chief constable returned from holiday.

The winning ladies were, from left, Mrs Bellamy, Mrs Spawson, Mrs Turnor, Mrs A Eatch, Mrs Burrows, Mrs Burdall and Mrs Barnes.

## Ladies win Eatch way

DYSART Park Ladies beat Wyndham Park to claim the Arthur Eatch Rose Bowl.

The annual bowls competition was played between the two parks, taking turns to be host club.

# Grantham in the News — 1930

## The talkies have arrived

TALKING pictures arrived at Grantham in May.

After exhaustive tests, Picture House proprietor John Campbell installed the British Thompson Houston sound system at great expense.

Mr Campbell said the days of having to read the story on the screen were a thing of the past.

He was looking at a similar system for the Empire Theatre, George Street.

The first film to be shown to packed houses was The Rainbow Man with Eddie Dowling and Frankie Darro.

Three days later was The Singing Fool starring Al Jolson.

The novelty meant a hike in prices. Trips to the cinema went up on average by 20 per cent.

The cost of sitting in the pit rose to 2.5p, the stalls 6p and the best seats at the front of the balcony shot up by 2p to 12p.

## Girls come out

DEBUTANTES Shelaugh and Crista de Paravicini, of St Vincent's, Grantham, were presented at their Majesties' Court, London, in May.

They wore identical long frocks of parchment coloured net with light satin bodices and pink net trains.

## Getting bigger

GRANTHAM grew by 1,000 hectares by absorbing land from neighbouring parishes. It doubled the size of the town.

A third of the expansion came from Spittlegate Without, while a quarter was by annexing much of Manthorpe.

Gonerby Hill Foot and parts of Barrowby and Old Somerby were also brought in the town boundary.

## Epidemic

THERE were 14 new cases of scarlet fever in January, causing the isolation hospital in Gorse Lane to be reopened. There were also 16 cases of chicken pox, mainly children.

## Getting rid of the rotten buses

THE introduction of mechanical inspections of buses in town was paying off, according to the chairman of the town's Watch Committee.

Coun Rothwell Lee said following the inspections, many defects had been corrected and several had been condemned and moved to other areas.

Most of the faults were badly adjusted brakes.

## Village boy Villa star

BILLINGBOROUGH sporting teenager Eric Houghton had an outstanding match for Aston Villa in their FA Cup tie against Reading.

Houghton was captain of Billingborough FC for a season before joining Boston Town.

After leaving school in 1928, he was capped for England against Scotland in a junior international at Edinburgh.

He made his debut for Villa's first team in 1929, while he was still under 20.

Billingborough had no lack of soccer heroes. Eric's uncle, Cecil Harris, had joined Villa three years earlier while another relative, Reg Goodacre, was with West Ham.

---

Now's the time to get your

**Chauntry Flannels**

Whatever the occasion - for sport or country - flannels are the thing nowadays - and the CHAUNTRY BRAND is the best. Made in a large variety of fittings, in grey and silver shades, they can be relied upon to wear well and always look smart, because they are cut in the latest fashion and fit perfectly.

Do not wait until the hot weather comes, get your CHAUNTRY FLANNELS now from

**F. W. SHEPPARD**
BOYS' & GENTLEMEN'S OUTFITTER
52 HIGH ST., GRANTHAM

# 1931 Grantham in the News

## Lucky Tom

THOMAS Beck of Inner Street, won £248 on the Peterborough Tote.

He selected the four most unlikely away wins, namely: Millwall, Walsall, Exeter and Queen's Park.

## Unlucky Tom

TOM Geeson, of Swayfield, was blown off his motorbike by a gust of wind as he rode past the end of Station Road East, along London Road, Grantham.

Red Cross men at Grantham FC's soccer match went to his aid.

He was then taken to Grantham Hospital by Dr Jocelyn Jauch.

## Ripped off

A FIFTEEN-year-old boy was questioned by police following the receipt by several Grantham women of threatening letters signed "Jack the Ripper".

## Catch of the day

NELL, a three-year-old terrier owned by R Elston, of Hand's Yard, Grantham, gave an astonishing display of rat-catching.

At Mr Stanton's garage, behind Pearke's Stores, Market Place, the bitch accounted for 81 rats in three hours.

## Well stuck

AN empty double-decker bus became wedged under Barrowby Road railway bridge, blocking both carriageways.

It was released by deflating the tyres.

## Woman's vitriol attack on her married lover

A GRANTHAM woman who threw acid into the face of her married lover, was cleared of all charges by Lincoln Assizes.

It happened on Christmas Eve after Rose Bontoft (33), of 17 Pretoria Road, went out with her neighbours John and Amy Dolby.

As they returned down the passage to the rear of their homes, with the Dolbys arm-in-arm, Mr Dolby turned his head to say goodbye.

Miss Bontoft flashed a torch into Mr Dolby's eyes dazzling him, then threw the vitriol.

Mr Dolby, a bricklayer, was taken to hospital where it was feared he may lose an eye.

His face was permanently scarred. The defence produced letters to the court, written to Miss Bontoft by Mr Dolby which showed the pair were on intimate terms.

Miss Bontoft said she had paid for the clothes he was wearing and only intended to ruin them. She did not mean to harm Mr Dolby.

The jury cleared Miss Bontoft of throwing the vitriol with intent to burn and was discharged.

## Death of top England ploughman

MILES Hardy, of 31 Wharf Road, Grantham, died in April aged 80.

He gained national fame as a ploughman, winning his first match at Bennington, near Boston, when he was only 16.

He went on to win six other leading championships that year.

He won his first England championship in 1875, the year he moved to Grantham from Friskney.

At the age of 72, he was still recognised as England's finest ploughman.

## Family hires charabanc for day trip

THE Tebb family, of Long Bennington, hired a charabanc for a day out to the coast.

The coach was owned by George Moyses, standing on the step, who owned the village coach business Silver Queen.

# Grantham in the News — 1931

## Unlucky strike wrecks range

A BOLT of lightning during a storm struck a chimney stack, bringing it crashing on to the slate roof of a Caythorpe house.

The bolt continued down the chimney into the kitchen ripping plaster off the walls, damaging the range and three kettles on it and throwing a wooden stool across the room.

Miss Scott, who was in the kitchen at the time, was struck between her wrist and elbow and on her cheek, causing her tongue to swell.

Upstairs a bedroom grate was shattered.

The storm which swept through the village also left several homes flooded to a depth of 70cm.

*Delighted children at Welby Street School*

## Improvements are trumps

WELBY Street School was refurbished.

Improvements included central heating and electric lighting.

A whist drive was held at Catlin's Cafe, High Street, where 83 people raised £6 towards the cost of improvements.

## Young woman dies in shooting accident

THE 21-year old daughter of a South Witham travelling showman died after being shot in the stomach.

Emily White was passing the loaded rifle to her father George at the family shooting gallery, when it went off.

The incident happened at Bitchfield, where the family was setting up the water balls shooting gallery.

She said: "Oh dad I've shot myself", walked about 25m and collapsed.

She died before Dr Koogh, of Corby, arrived 20 minutes later.

Recording accidental death he coroner warned her father to be more careful in future.

## New homes to cost up to 60p a week

FIFTY-TWO houses being built on Signal Road were nearing completion.

They departed from the usual Grantham design, with metal casements instead of traditional wood sash-windows. The red brick was softened by white cement stucco.

The basic design was Georgian influence with some doorways finished with pediments. They were also designed to catch maximum sunshine. Rents were set between 45p and 60p a week.

The new road linking Signal Road to Hill Avenue was called Gorse Rise, to reflect the importance of the shrub on Harrowby Hills.

The gorse, however, was expected to disappear under further developments.

## Woman jailed for fraud

A WOMAN who got food and lodgings valued at 60p under false pretences was jailed by Grantham magistrates for three months with hard labour.

She had asked Carrie George, of Manthorpe Road, if she could stay a few nights as her husband was in Grantham Hospital following a road accident at Foston.

But Mrs George was suspicious and notified the police.

When Pc Ledger arrested May Wilson, of no fixed abode, he found the story about her husband was a pack of lies.

Police then discovered there were warrants out for her in other towns including Barnsley, Doncaster, Chesterfield, Leeds, Mansfield, Retford and Newark.

# 1931 Grantham in the News

## Factory closure boosts jobless figures

UNEMPLOYMENT broke the 2,100 barrier for the first time.

A total of 2,058 men were out of work, made up of 1,665 men, 99 boys, 197 women and 97 girls.

British Corosit Button Company's factory closure after only a year in town accounted for 100 jobs and dismissals at Ruston and Hornsby continued to swell the figure.

## Town chairman quits

THE annual meeting of Grantham Football Club was told gate receipts for the season had dropped from £2,099 in 1930 to £1,669 this year.

But wages also fell to £1,582 compared with £1,996 the previous season. During the season 50,000 spectators went through the turnstiles.

Transfers provided £705 net and the supporters club donated £179.

Chairman Arthur Eatch announced his retirement. He said: "It's time for a change.

"I have a lot of work commitments and I don't get pleasure from the club anymore."

Mr R Bell was appointed chairman.

## Death of Brownlow's heir

THE Hon David Peregrine Cust, infant son and heir to Lord and Lady Brownlow, died at Belton House, six days after his first birthday.

The borough flag was flown at half mast over the Guildhall.

He was the first direct heir born to the Brownlow succession for 90 years.

Their surviving child was the Hon Caroline Cust, aged two.

## Bus company expands

GREAT Gonerby-based bus company Simmonds Bros became licensed to run a daily service from Grantham to Ropsley, Great Gonerby, Bourne, Corby, Barrowby and Irnham.

But the Traffic Commissioners told them they must end their service from Grantham to Skegness.

They also refused permission for bus trips to Nottingham Goose Fair following objections by Trent Motor Traction Company.

## Saving cash

GRANTHAM Borough Council decided not to give any rises to its staff this year as it was carrying out cost-cutting exercises.

---

**MELIAS**

"FAR LESS THAN I EXPECTED TO SPEND"

Many Customers have been agreeably surprised at the Modest Cost of their Weekly Purchases of Grocery and Provisions, also the quick and efficient service at

**MELIAS**

BUTCHERING DEPARTMENT NOW OPEN

CHOICE SELECTION
CHILLED LAMB AND CHILLED BEEF
AT PRICES THAT
SAVE YOU PENCE PER LB

BACON REDUCED AGAIN.

| BEST PALE SIDE SLICED 6d. PER LB | FINEST REFINED LARD 5d PER LB. | LEAN PALE GAMMON SLICED 1/- PER LB |

Finest EMPIRE BUTTER Reduced to 1/1 per lb.

| DELICIOUS Margerine REDUCED to per 5d lb. | FINEST Empire Cheese REDUCED to per 7d. lb. |

Finest White Flour 1/2 Per Stone

AGENTS FOR
**DOMINION TEA** 7D PER 1/4 LB.
Free Life Insurance
Free Gifts
ENQUIRE FOR PARTICULARS AND FREE GIFT BOOKLET

**MELIAS** 8, MARKET PLACE GRANTHAM

# Grantham in the News — 1931

## Milkman slips up

MILKMAN Harry Exton was injured while delivering milk along Wharf Road.

He jumped from his horse-drawn dray to deliver a bottle to a nearby house, when he slipped beneath it.

Both the front and back wheels ran over his legs.

But he had a lucky escape. Dr John Allan said no bones were broken, although the guiders were strained.

He said Mr Exton, of Charles Street, would recover with a rest.

## Birds restricted

YOUTH Hector Dolby, of New Street, was fined 50p for keeping linnets in a cage which was too small to stretch their wings.

RSPCA inspector Curley said he saw two youths catching wild birds with nets at Gonerby Hill Foot.

There were two cages, 15cm by 13cm by 15cm each containing a linnet. The tips of the wings and the tail of one bird were broken.

## Baby boys killed by mad mother

A MOTHER who drowned her two sons in the River Witham was detained during her Majesty's pleasure by Lincolnshire Assizes.

Katie Annie Spouge (31), of Foston, was found guilty, of murdering Thomas (19 months) and Peter (7 months) but insane.

A charge of attempted murder of her daughter Gwendoline (4) was dropped.

Her mother-in-law was worried when the family failed to return home from a walk. She went to the river and saw Spouge holding the little girl under the water.

She rescued the child, but then saw the other two bodies near the sheep dip.

Dr Wilkie, of Long Bennington, said: "Mrs Spouge is in a state of dementure. She considered what she did was right."

At the same spot in June, Joseph E Stephenson and cripple Freda Thane died in a suicide pact.

## Tailor blames losing his hat for his drunkenness

A TAILOR charged with being drunk and disorderly blamed losing his hat for getting inebriated.

Walter Currall, from Sleaford, was seen in the Market Place area of Grantham, singing, swearing and waving his arms about, knocking two pedestrians off the pavement.

Police said he was warned several times before his arrest.

Currall (60) told Grantham Police Court: "I had a small drop of beer but I do not swear. I am usually of a sober disposition. I lost my hat and the sun affected my head."

Magistrates fined him 50p.

## Signals installed

TRAFFIC signals being installed in Grantham were improving safety and cutting the need for policemen on point duty.

They were put up at Brook Street-Swinegate crossroads, the Angel and Royal and Bridge End Road.

But not everyone welcomed them. One townsman said: "It gets more like London every day."

## Gloomy night

GRANTHAM Thursday Wolves lodged a protest over the result of their Thursday Swiss Shield match against Notts Co-op.

After 90 minutes, the score was goalless but in extra time, in complete darkness, Co-op scored the deciding goal.

*London Road where car parking was said to be blocking traffic flows.*

## Traffic forcing rethink on London Road

DEMANDS were made in the town for land to be found for additional car parking.

London Road was especially bad, with buses and lorries, blocking the flow of traffic, according to a town council survey.

# 1931 Grantham in the News

## Market gardener jailed for blackmailing gamekeeper

A STUBTON man was jailed for three years for demanding £50 with menaces.

Market gardener George Parker (29) was found guilty by Nottingham Assizes.

He demanded cash from Fenton gamekeeper Harry Chapman, to stop spreading rumours about him and a respectable young lady.

Parker told Mr Chapman, head gamekeeper at Stubton Hall, the young woman was his fiancee.

He claimed she was pregnant and demanded £100 or he would tell everyone Mr Chapman was the father.

He later brought his demand down to £50.

The lady said she never had a child and although friendly with Parker, had never been engaged to him.

## Shaw's goes bust

MR Hollinton of Leicester was appointed liquidator of long-time Grantham company Shaw's Tanneries, of Earlesfield Lane.

Another receiver appointed earlier in the year said the company was not viable and only managed to dispose of some of the stock.

The company had employed 170 people.

**C. E. FENSOM**
HIGH-CLASS FAMILY
**BUTCHER**
18, HIGH STREET,
GRANTHAM

*If in doubt TRY FENSOM, where Quality excels*

*The new building*

## Cheers! Drinkers like the new Five Bells

THE old Five Bells, Brook Street, was demolished and a new building erected in its place.

The nearby Three Crowns, Manthorpe Road, was closed for good.

Built by Arthur Eatch & Son, the new building was designed to fit in with neighbouring Georgian properties and was faced with Stamford stone.

It was fitted with the latest metal windows.

It was set back three metres from the pavement with a paved forecourt.

## Grantham shrinking - official

THE 10-year census showed Grantham's population had fallen over the past 20 years, even though the area had trebled in size.

In April it was discovered the town had 19,630 residents compared to 20,070 in 1911.

The fall was blamed on the closure of the Ministry of Pensions Hospital, on Harrowby Camp.

In the same period, both Newark and Melton Mowbray had grown by more than 1,000.

# Grantham in the News — 1931

## Jailed for incident at Hungerton

JOHN Fisher, of Nottingham was jailed for dangerous driving and failing to stop for a policeman.

He was spotted by Pc Sargent and a gamekeeper standing outside Hungerton Hall, with a man on his running board brandishing a gun.

The constable stepped into the road and signalled for him to stop, but was forced to jump clear as the car sped on.

Gamekeeper Mr Hollingsworth threw a stick which smashed the car's windscreen.

The car then crashed through a five-bar gate.

When arrested Fisher insisted the gamekeeper should be charged for the damage he caused.

He said he didn't see the constable. He said: "All I saw was the gamekeeper running towards me with a stick and smashing it through the windscreen.

"I got glass in my eyes and was blinded."

Fisher was jailed for two months for dangerous driving and fined 50p for failing to stop.

## Award for stay maker

MISS Ada Hodson, of 36 St Peter's Hill, Grantham, was presented with a gold badge recognising 20 years as a Spirella corsetiere.

More than 1,000 corsetieres turned out for the company's 21st birthday celebrations.

**Watergate preparing for road-widening scheme**

## More traffic leads to call for widening

AFTER declaring Watergate unfit for modern traffic, the borough council revealed plans for a widening scheme.

There would be a 40ft line preventing any future development inside it, to allow for further improvements in the future.

Three buildings at the top of the road would have to be demolished. They were D H Sharpley, J S Stanton and the Strathdon Hotel.

The footpath from Vine Street was to be at least three metres wide.

A council spokesman said: "There may have to be some compromises and it may take time to come to fruition."

## Read about it

THERE were 2,801 adult members of Grantham Public Library, an increase of 210 over the previous year.

They borrowed 72,813 books. Junior members amounted to 989, borrowing 16,705 books.

## Smokers

BUS drivers Eric Staples, of Claypole, and Victor Jarman, of Long Bennington, appeared before Newark Magistrates charged with smoking while driving.

They were discharged on payment of costs.

## New council

GRANTHAM Rural District Council became West Kesteven RDC.

Extra parishes from the Claypole area brought the total in the new area to 51.

## Bill for road

HOUSEHOLDERS in Hill Avenue, a private road, received a massive bill from the borough council, which carried out road repairs after residents failed to.

## Whoopee! It's open

THE theatre in George Street re-opened as the Theatre Royal and Empire Cinema following a major facelift.

The building was decorated throughout with more comfortable seats.

Then able to show films too, it opened with Whoopee, starring Eddie Cantor.

# 1932 Grantham in the News

## Third jobless

UNEMPLOYMENT in the Grantham area averaged 36.2 per cent of the insured population. This was well above the 22.2 per cent national figure.

## Blue Horse rebuilt

THE Blue Horse Inn, Great Ponton, was again open for business. The previous property having already been pulled down, the impressive new building was faced with Sileby brick with Weldon stone windows and leaded lights.

## Service report

BETWEEN 800 and 1,000 worshippers turned out for the three-hour service at St John's Church, Spittlegate, for the Good Friday service.

## Stolen milk

A RESIDENT of Rugby Cottages, was fined 50p for stealing a pint of milk from the step of the Bank Buildings, Butchers Row, Grantham.

He said he had an invalid wife and he was distraught at having to look after the children.

It was his first offence.

## Mowbeck clean up

FIFTY-TWO loads of silt were taken out of the Mowbeck during a clean up.

It was agreed to build two settling tanks in Golding's yard, Old Wharf Road, at a cost of £40 to ease the problem in future.

*New showroom under construction*

## Motor Company expands

GRANTHAM Motor Company, London Road, was expanding.

The Ford dealer, which also sold tractors, built a new showroom for the agricultural side of its businesss, at the foot of Somerby Hill.

The new company, Grantham Tractor Company, was a Fordson dealership.

## First motorists fined for ignoring town's traffic signals

GRANTHAM'S 'robot policemen', the new automatic traffic signals at four junctions in the town, became 'humanised'.

Under new regulations authorised by the Ministry of Transport it became an offence to ignore them.

The first batch of offenders was dealt with by magistrates when seven summonses were heard

Three of them were women.

All six offences were committed on March 25 at the Market Place - Watergate junction.

In each case it was claimed the driver could not see the lights because of the heavy traffic in front of them. They were each fined 50p.

## Summer arrives with a vengeance

A SUMMER heatwave arrived in Grantham with temperatures creating tropical conditions for two weeks.

In the town centre, temperatures reached 28 degrees Celsius in the shade.

The coolest place was the open-air swimming baths where hundreds turned out. At both Wyndham Park and Dysart Park baths, about 1,400 people turned out for a dip on one day alone.

## New dustbins

BOROUGH councillors agreed to buy new dustbins for their their council tenants at a cost of 42.5p each.

# Grantham in the News — 1932

## Record rainfall swamps town

TWO storms in three days in July brought havoc to the town.

On the last Monday of the month, 7cm of rain fell and on Wednesday, 9cm.

By Thursday, more than 18cm had fallen.

In the area at the foot of Dysart Road and Wharf Road, floods were half-a-metre deep.

Flooding under Springfield Road railway bridge made the road impassable. Sewers failed to cope with the heavy rainfall and discharged into the streets.

Heavy manhole covers were blown off and traffic was brought to a halt in case vehicles fell down any holes.

Streets around Wyndham Park escaped the worst as the new sewer managed to cope.

A 'tramp bus' collected people stranded in their homes.

**Pumping out on Wharf Road**

## Union men call for a shorter working week

GRANTHAM Trades Council leader called for a shorter working week.

George Ancliffe said the time had come for a five-day week of 40 hours. He also called for the abolition of means testing.

Addressing a crowded meeting in the Westgate Hall, he said: "If unemployment is to be solved, there must be a shorter working week.

"If we are not alert, machines will crush both masters and men."

Town councillor William Goodliff also called for the end of means testing.

He said: "In this town there are glaring instances of injustice."

Mr Berry, of the AEU, said: "Machines should be the servant of man, not his master.

"Seventy-five per cent more boots are now produced than in 1914 yet fewer men were employed and more men, women and children were ill-shod and shoeless."

### Father's Jubilee

FATHER Leo Arendsen was presented with £75 by parishioners to celebrate his 25 years as a priest.

A promising artist, he had been at St Mary's Church, Grantham, for 18 years. A party was held at the Clarion Cafe, Market Place, after a Sunday evening service.

## Heavyweight attraction

THE 'Big Noise' of boxing, Italian heavyweight Primo Carnera, paid a visit to Grantham.

The controversial boxer, the tallest in the sport's history, called at the Corner House Cafe before catching his train to London.

He ate a hearty breakfast of bacon and eggs which he washed down with a litre of milk.

This was followed by a litre of water.

The 203cm tall boxer weighing in at 124kg was on his way from Nottingham where he had given an exhibition at the New Victoria Hall.

## Unlimited parking led to obstructions

SINCE unlimited parking was abolished on St Peter's Hill, parking in Grantham High Street began to cause obstructions, Grantham Town Council was told.

It was resolved in fututre that parking, would be restricted to one hour, on St Peter's Hill, Market Place (except on Saturdays) and Wide Westgate.

Twenty minute restrictions would apply to all other streets except the narrow part of High Street and Watergate where it was banned.

37

# 1932 Grantham in the News

## Good bet for gambling ban

A COUNCILLOR'S move to ban the Globe of Death, games of chance and shows involving the torture of animals at the Mid-Lent Fair, were backed by the Town Council.

But while adopting Coun Alfred Robert's motion, Coun Holmes, chairman of the markets, fairs and lighting committee, said personally he saw no harm in any of them.

Meanwhile, church leaders called on the town council to keep an eye on amusements at the fair.

They said too many games of chance were appearing, which were corrupting the young.

Vicar of Grantham Canon Markham said: "It would be a thousand pities if the young got bitten with the passion for money-making and developed a passion for betting and gambling.

"They now come away with money jingling in their pockets, whereas before it was coconuts and weirdly-coloured vases."

## Death and injuries in the fog

A MOTORCYCLIST died and two men were badly burned in one day during dense fog.

Engine driver Frederick Asprey (30), of Bridge End Road, was killed when he collided with a Reliance bus on Somerby Hill.

The bus radiator was smashed in the collision.

Earlier in the day, a lorry carrying groceries and provisions ran into the trailer of another truck coming down Spittlegate Hill. The lorry burst into flames leaving the two men in the cab with serious burns.

The lorry and its contents were destroyed in the blaze.

## Tim's Grand homecoming

FLAGS and bunting festooned Alexandra Road, to welcome home Grantham's sporting hero jockey Tim Hamey.

The 26-year-old who won the Grand National on 50-1 outsider Forbra, returned to his home town to visit his parents.

## Showman dies in trailer fall

A TRAVELLING showman who fell out of the back of a trailer at Corby, died of his injuries.

Witnesses say they heard a crash but no other vehicles were on the road at the time.

Village GP Dr H N Witham said George Leveson Jackson (47), of Sleaford, died of a broken neck and probably died instantly.

## Month in jail for indecent assault

A NINETEEN-year-old Grantham man admitted indecently assaulting two girls aged seven and eight.

He said he did not know what he was doing.

Sentencing him to one month in jail, magistrate Tryner Lynn said: "You have a bad record and are old enough to know better.

"I must give you a sentence which would be an advantage to you in later life."

## Roman furnace uncovered

A RARE Roman blast furnace was uncovered by workmen clearing a fall in Colsterworth ironstone quarry.

The metre-square clay structure was found with pottery and slag in place.

The find was cleared and left exposed for four days to be photographed.

Unfortunately, several frosts took their toll and the structure crumbled into dust.

---

LET

**MAISON META**

SOLVE YOUR

Millinery Problems

Newest Styles in the Latest Coarse Straw
at
3/11. 5/11, 6/11, 8/11, 9/11, 12/11.

23, St. Peter's Hill

# Grantham in the News  1932

## Hunger marchers are well supported by townsfolk

ABOUT 150 hunger marchers from the North-East shipyards and mining districts trudged into Grantham footsore but cheerful.

They were accompanied by the rattle of drums and the strains of a piano-accordion.

Carrying bold red banners, they were among contingents from all over England threading their way to a mass demonstration in London to protest against the means test.

They had to beg their food and spent many nights sleeping in workhouses, but they received a cordial welcome in Grantham.

They were taken to the Westgate Hall where they stayed overnight with blankets loaned by the public assistance committee. Meals were served at the Co-op.

At Foston, John Smith of Newcastle, one of the oldest marchers, was knocked down by a motor ambulance and one of his legs was broken.

## Police force pubs to shut

TWO public houses the Star and Garter, Castlegate, and the Welby Arms, Welby Street, were shut down as redundant.

Chief Constable Casburn told the licensing court the Star and Garter had 12 other public houses within 200 metres including the Beehive almost next door and the Blue Cow 40 metres away.

This area of town had 127 people per licensed premise compared with 259 in the rest of the borough.

Star and Garter tenant, Mrs Vessey, said she scarcely scraped a living.

The Welby Arms, said Mr Casburn, had 25 on-licences within 200 metres including the Plough, Peacock and Durham Ox in the same street.

There was one pub for every 86 residents in the area.

## Luck of Irish

A BLACK kitten which strolled into the Picture House cinema, St Peter's Hill, brought good luck for two girls working in the pay desk.

Instead of evicting it from the premises, they gave it a saucer of milk and nursed it.

Two hours later the two girls discovered they had won a share in the £100 prize of the Irish Sweepstake.

## Fowl move at village whist drive

MISS Benson and Mrs Wilson tied in the Billingborough whist drive for choral society funds, in which the first prize was a chicken for the table.

And when they refused to cut cards for the top prize, organisers decided to cut the prize by chopping the fowl into two and giving them half each.

**The lorry parks up outside the Blue Horse, London Road.**

## Steady as she goes for ship's rudder

GRANTHAM traffic came to a standstill when the largest construction in the world to be transported by lorry passed through the town.

The lorry was on its way from the North-East to Southampton carrying a repaired rudder for the SS Berengaria.

The lorry had travelled northwards to Darlington, the previous week.

At 9am the vehicle stopped at the Blue Horse, on London Road, for the driver and mates to have breakfast while crowds of sightseers turned out to see the unusual spectacle.

The 55-tonne rudder needed a 150-tonne crane to lift it into position at Southampton docks having been transported on the 650-mile round trip by the world's biggest lorry.

# 1932 Grantham in the News

## Huntsmen see death-defying air crash

RIDERS out with the Belvoir Hunt, at Three Queens, Croxton Kerrial, witnessed an RAF plane crashing into a tree at high speed.

And they were even more surprised when the pilot climbed free with minor injuries.

Pilot Officer Le Borgne, stationed at Grantham Aerodrome, had been one of two pilots entertaining the field with an aerial display including looping-the-loop.

The pilot was taken to Grantham Hospital and said to be making good progress.

## Cricket club closes after 50 years

AT a meeting held at the Crown Inn, it was decided to wind up Billingborough Cricket Club after half a century.

The reason given was lack of support and interest, confirmed by the fact that only six people turned up for the meeting.

## Ex-Soldier tells wife "Go away. I don't want you!"

A DISABLED ex-soldier told magistrates he did not want his wife, the mother of his seven surviving children.

Florence Dodwell, living in a caravan in Blue Lion Yard, said she had two young girls with her while a young son lived with his father.

She said Charles Dodwell refused to give her any money from his £3.67 per week pension.

She said: "He turned me out with a baby in my arms undressed."

Mr Dodwell said he paid her every week, keeping nothing back.

A neighbour told magistrates Mrs Dodwell seemed to get on his nerves.

Mr Dodwell was ordered to pay her £1 a week.

## Plough for sale

THE Plough Inn, Welby Street, was bought by Spalding brewers Soames for £1,850.

William Liddiard, of Wilsford, bought both his village pub, and the Plough at the sale.

## Speeders caught

FOLLOWING a check by police on a six-mile stretch of the Great North Road south of Long Bennington, three lorry drivers were fined.

They all exceeded the road's 15mph speed limit.

## Epidemic spotted in the area

SIXTY-seven case of chicken pox were reported in the first two months of the year as the epdiemic swept through the Grantham area.

This was far higher than the whole of the year previous when there were only 43 cases.

Health officials were concerned that a mild form of the more serious small pox could be diagnosed as chicken pox.

Health committee chairman Ald Rawle said he was not concerned as it was a mild complaint.

## Council cuts roadmen's pay

COUNCIL roadmen were forced to take a pay cut as the cash-strapped town council were forced to make economies.

Their wages were slashed by 10p bringing their weekly wage down to £1.50.

Opposing the move, Coun Jones said most men paid 34p rent and 4p National Insurance which did not leave a living wage.

---

It is well known that

**Fyffe's Blue Label Bananas**

Ripened by

**STERNE AUSTIN**

are unbeatable.

His TOBACCO DEPARTMENT

is dainty and inviting

23a, ST. PETER'S HILL

# Grantham in the News 1933

## Pilot escapes hanger crash

AN aircraft taking off from RAF Spitalgate crashed into one of the hangers, destroying both.

There were no casualties.

Pilot Officer W Ellborough was taking off in an Armstrong Whitworth Siskin when it crashed into the roof of the hanger.

The wings remained in the roof while the fuselage fell to the floor.

Within minutes, the hanger, which was built in the First World War, was ablaze and razed to the ground. Both pilot and airmen working in the building escaped uninjured.

**The scene at RAF Spittlegate after the crash**

## Firm brings job prospects

A DEAL between Ruston and Hornsby, Barford and Perkins and Aveling Porter found work for unemployed engineers.

The land on Houghton Road became the new home for Aveling Barford, which moved its road roller manufacturing from Rochester.

Grantham firm Parks and Son won the £6,000 contract to build new offices, a two-storey office block measuring 60m by 12m.

It was near two large workshops taken over from Ruston and Hornsby.

Most plant was brought by rail and 150 key men were transferred from Kent.

A garden village called Walton Gardens was built off Springfield Road to house 120 families.

Situated east of Rudd's brickyard, the plot was occupied by allotments at the bottom and pasture at the top. It was on a 23-metre slope and a public footpath was diverted.

## Tragic death of Horbling farm worker

A HORBLING farm worker was killed when a lorry skidded and crashed into his cart.

Tom Picker was carting sugar beet to a clamp at Bridge End when the accident happened.

Mr Picker (60) was tossed forward over the horse's head, the horse bolted, and a cart wheel was pulled over his chest.

He had only recently celebrated his Golden Wedding.

He had worked on the land since he was seven years old, when he earned 2.5p a day. Aged 10, he was working a 12-hour day.

## Coarse Language

A GRANTHAM man living in Blue Ram Yard, was fined £1 by Borough Magistrates for swearing at his wife.

The couple lived in a caravan and their rows could be clearly heard.

The man said his wife had provoked him with claims that he had another woman.

## No new name

AN application to the town council to change the name of Chamber's Yard, Norton Street, to Scoffield's Cottages was refused.

## Demands for pensions at 60

A MEETING in Grantham Sessions Hall called for pensions to be paid at 60 to reduce unemployment.

The meeting followed a talk in the town earlier in the year by the National Association for Pensions at Sixty.

Grantham was the first town to set up a branch.

The Rev R F Skinner said: "About 200 turned up for a lively meeting. Membership of the branch has now doubled to more than 80."

He said when pensions of 25p a week were paid to over-70s it was said the country would go bankrupt.

41

# 1933 Grantham in the News

## Weather report - it's wet and dry

THE Grantham Canal was frozen for several days in January, the start of a crazy year of weather.

By the end of February, Grantham was in the grip of a great blizzard which swept through the country.

Traffic was brought to a halt for several days with hundreds of cars snowed up and many villages cut off.

In compensation, a brilliant summer followed. Swimming pools were invaded by record crowds and opening hours were extended.

The August rainfall was 1.3mm, the lowest on record.

The drought continued into the winter months with a very dry December, which forced the water company to publish notices warning about leaks and wastage.

The only breach in the drought was a fall of snow in October.

*Civic leaders meet Burton's bosses at the new menswear shop*

## Suitable architecture for new store

A MEN'S clothing shop opened at the corner of High Street and Market Place.

The new purpose-built shop for Montague Burton was regarded as a valuable addition to the town's architecture.

Work on the interior should have been carried out by Mr W Case, of Leicester, who measured up and ordered the fittings, but he died before they were delivered.

## Two-year-old dies of scalding

A TWO-year-old died of scalding after falling into a bucket of water her mother had prepared for washing.

Gladys Gray, of Marston, had run into the kitchen, where the bucket was, with some dolls' clothes for rinsing.

## Pawnbrokers hit

A CONSIDERABLE amount of jewellery was stolen from pawnbrokers Smith and Warren, Castlegate.

Thieves entered through a house at the rear, owned by greengrocer Mr C L Smith, who was with his wife at Harrowby Methodist Church.

## Births rates up

BIRTHS at 331 for the year were up 31 on the previous year.

There were 247 deaths, including eight from cancer, three from influenza, two from whooping cough and one from appendicitis.

The death rate of under-ones was half the national average.

## Beetle causes the death of an angel

A HAMMER beam angel was removed from the roof, north of the Corpus Christi Chapel in St Wulfram's, Grantham.

Serious damage at the base was found to be caused by death watch beetle.

# Grantham in the News — 1933

## Royal visit gives heart to Grantham's jobless

PRINCE George, youngest son of the King, visited Grantham and spent an hour seeing how the unemployed took advantage of the welfare schemes.

The Prince talked to the men for 30 minutes getting their views on the scheme, run by the National Council of Social Service.

He studied how institutions were 'combating the evil effects of idleness'.

He saw the Occupational Club in the Market Place and the Recreational Club.

At the Prince's request, the visit was informal.

He was anxious to know how the schemes operated and how the men coped with enforced leisure.

Prince George chatted in a homely manner taking an interest in their work and how they felt.

He seemed to be deeply concerned after hearing each man's story and won a warm place in their hearts by his kindly and friendly manner.

## Power mad Billingborough

BILLINGBOROUGH was in turmoil as the Mid-Lincolnshire Electrical Supply Company dug up the streets to bring power to the village.

A metre deep trench was dug down Church Street, High Street and Station Road, from the transformer supplied by an overhead HT cable being erected on Folkingham Road.

About 20 extra unemployed men from the area were set on to speed up the work.

## Train tragedy

A PACKING-CASE maker from Grantham died of his injuries after attempting to board a moving train.

Bernard Anderton Le Hair (36), of Agnes Terrace, was returning from Victoria Station, London, with his brother Charles, when the train stopped at High Level station, Nottingham.

He left the train to use the station toilet.

As the train pulled away, Mr Le Hair ran after it.

His brother held the door open but as he entered the compartment he slipped between the carriage and the platform.

## Licence less

ARTHUR Hadley of Artichokes Yard, Swinegate, was fined 50p by town magistrates for failing to have a licence for his wireless apparatus.

**The Midland Bank is demolished to make way for Marks & Spencer**

## The old makes way for new

THE Midland Bank, High Street was pulled down together with Foster's tobacconist.

In their place, national clothing store Marks & Spencer built a new shop, opened in August, where nothing cost more than 25p.

During the demolition, an old wall, more than two metres thick and made of rubble, was discovered.

The wall, believed to be part of a building that stood on the site 600 years ago, was demolished for use as foundations of the new store.

Charming masonry with mullion windows in the passage by the Maypole shop were also destroyed to make way for the development.

The bank transferred its business to Westgate.

43

# 1933 Grantham in the News

## Paint job

THE contract for painting the exteriors of the new houses in Gorse Rise and Signal Road was awarded to G Beech and Son. The tender was worth £81.70.

## Dog with no name

A GRANTHAM man was fined 25p by magistrates for failing to have his name and address on the collar of his dog.

## Lorries collide

TWO lorries crashed on Spittlegate Hill, destroying the wall of a urinal.

## Silence in court

CASES at Spittlegate Sessions had to be adjourned because of the lack of policemen.
 Only one summons could be dealt with because officers required as witnesses in other cases were victims of the influenza epidemic.

## Unemployment falls

FIGURES issued in December showed Grantham's jobless was down to 1,600.
This was a vast improvement on the 2,350 at the start of the year.

## Bus station is open

THE Mayor's wife, Mrs Forsgate Weekley, opened the new bus station between Welham Street and St Peter's Hill.
 A kiosk for fruit and other refreshments was let to Pulford and Sons as a convenience for passengers.

*The tractor outside the Post Office, St Peter's Hill*

## Tractor barges through town

AN iron dredging barge hauled by a Fowler B6 road locomotive brought traffic to a standstill in October.

The boat, made by Gwynnes Pumps of Lincoln, was on its way to London. Although railway operator LNER was charged with the move, it was far too big to move by rail.

The cargo was too big to bring through Chapel Street and had to go by Brownlow Street and Broad Street before turning on to the Great North Road in North Street to continue its journey through town.

## Pilot killed in Ponton crash

A PILOT from Croydon died after his aircraft crashed into a field at Little Ponton in fog.

George Watson (27) received severe injuries and died of shock in Grantham Hospital.
 He had remained conscious throughout.

Mr Watson gave air displays and had stayed overnight at the town's George Hotel.
 Joseph Cox, who was seeding cabbages at the time, heard the aircraft crash.

He went to the scene of the accident some 50 metres away and helped to get the pilot out.

Ernest Atter, who was working with Mr Cox, said the "plane struck the ground terribly hard."

*Buy your Piano NOW*

THEY HAVE NEVER BEEN CHEAPER, BETTER, OR MORE VARIED

**WHITE AND SENTANCE,**
The Piano Stores,
GRANTHAM AND MELTON.

# Grantham in the News  1933

## Water shortage hits fire brigade

A SHORTAGE of water impeded Grantham Fire Brigade, who were called out six times in a fortnight.

At one call, The Pines, Ponton Heath, the nearest water was a pond in Stoke Hollow, a mile away.

Their pumps could not find enough pressure to pump up the hill, some 30 metres. They could only supervise as the fire burned itself out.

Thirty tonnes of clover and 45 tonnes of bale straw were destroyed together with a farm cart.

At Alford Street, Grantham, the pump was not required. They put out a sitting room blaze with buckets of water.

The following day, a lorry fire at the bottom of Gonerby Hill was allowed to burn when firemen discovered the village pond was dry.

### Seeing red

LORRY driver Leslie Fry, from Doncaster, was fined £1 for failing to illuminate his number plate.

Spittlegate Magistrates said his use of a hurricane lamp with a pink rag tied around the glass was not acceptable.

## Harry's lofty ideals

ASKING for a pint at a pub isn't usually a tall order but it was at the Horse and Jockey.

Serving the tall man is landlord Harry Palethorpe with his wife Kate looking on.

The man on stilts was from a circus visiting town.

## Woman killed by lightning strike

WINIFRED Watmore, of Vere Court, Grantham, died after being struck by lightning. The 21-year-old was one of a party of 23 men and women working in the fields for Mr Burtt, of Dowsby.

Four women were sheltering behind some barrels when it struck.

Two were slightly hit but Miss Watmore was struck on the head.

She was unconscious with blood seeping from her ears. She died the following day in Bourne Hospital.

## Black ice in schoolroom

FEBRUARY'S frosts were so keen, children at Spittlegate School arrived to find the ink had frozen in the inkwells.

It had to be thawed out in front of a fire before lessons could begin.

---

### If you had Eyes like a Cat

Contrary to popular belief a cat's eyes are not so sensitive or efficient as human eyes. But human eyes are oftenb allowed to deteriorate through overstrain. You can insure against this by having your eyes regularly examined and by wearing properly prescribed glasses as soon as they become necessaryin th best interest of your most precious asset - the gift of vision.

Consult

**Geo. E. Whysall**
SIGHT-TESTING OPTICA
High Street
GRANTHAM
Registered for National Health Insurance Work

---

45

# 1934     Grantham in the News

## Telephone boxes

THE town council approved plans by Post Office Telephones to erect kiosks on South Parade and at the corner of Station Road and Harlaxton Road.

## Milk watered down

AN Ingoldsby farmer was fined £2 for adulterating milk.

An analysis showed a churn, from which he was selling, contained 28 per cent water.

## Hospital cup winner

THE Hospital Cup for the licensee collecting the biggest sum in a year for Grantham Hospital was retained by Mr F A Steele of the Black Dog.

His customers raised £26.06, just 90p more than in 1933.

## Some truck

THE world's largest lorry, a Ransome and Rapier 480, capable of carrying up to 100 tonnes, passed through Grantham on its way to Scunthorpe.

## Eggceptional

DURING Egg Week in town 1,112 eggs plus £2.20 in cash went to inmates of the Poor Law Institution, Dysart Road. It was organised by ladies of the Guardian committee.

## Bus driver fined

A NEWCASTLE bus driver was fined £5 and had his licence endorsed for driving a coach through Little Ponton at speeds of up to 45mph.

## Six hundred turn out to hear Fascist leader's speech

FASCIST leader Sir Oswald Mosley attracted about 600 people who listened to the gospel of this post-war creed at an open air meeting in Wide Westgate, Grantham.

Among the audience were members of all political parties and a number of prominent farmers.

Watching from an overlooking window was Grantham Conservatives president Lord Brownlow with Lady Brownlow.

Sir Oswald made his address from a dray draped in the Union Flag.

He was given a fair, uninterrupted hearing, and the speech was free from hecklers.

He was accompanied by a party of his Blackshirts.

He said the Blackshirt movement was a loyal one, to both the King and country which wanted to bring about the changes necessary to build a nation worthy of the love of patriots.

He said: "We will take the lead in building peace in Europe but we cannot be the only unarmed nation among armed ones.

"This does not mean that we want war. To say that Fascism leads to war is nonsense."

## Top jockey injured

TIM Hamey, the Grantham-based steeplechase jockey, was injured in a spectacular fall at the Crowhurst Hurdle Race.

His mount, Salfora, fell full length although Tim managed to remain seated.

He was only slightly hurt.

## Boys fined for stone-throwing

SIX young boys were fined 20p each by Belvoir Magistrates for throwing stones at a railway engine.

Fireman Horace Hedworth told the court the attack was on the Grantham to Leicester train near Barkston.

He said they broke the spectacle glass in the locomotive cab and pieces could have hit him in the face had he been shovelling coal at the time.

---

**NEW SPRING MILLINERY**

at

Sharpley's

First with the New Styles — always! SHARPLEY'S now introduce the most fascinating MILLINERY MODELS for Spring. A delightful selection in the Latest Colours, and suitable for immediate wear. Just call and see them!

**D. & H. Sharpley**

"Nº 1" HIGH STREET GRANTHAM

# Grantham in the News 1934

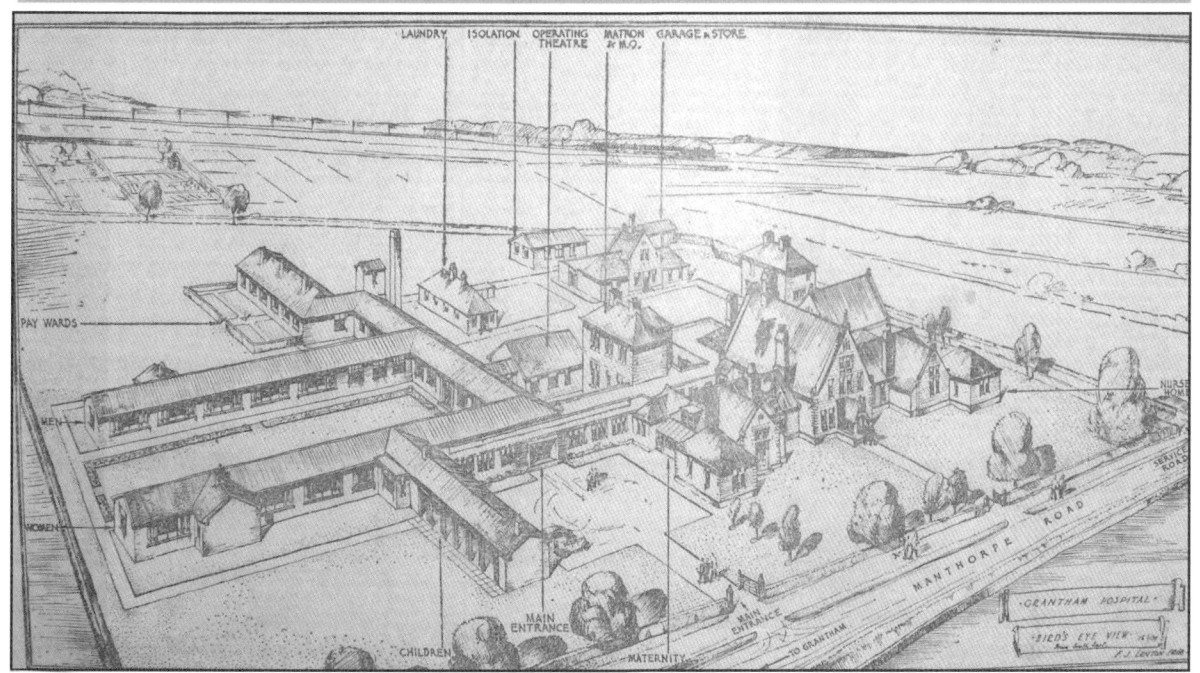

*Planned expansion for the town's hospital*

## Massive hospital expansion scheme

BUILDER Bernard Pumfrey was awarded the contract for extensions at Grantham Hospital.

Its tender for £18,787 was several hundred pounds cheaper than the second best of nine received.

The new buildings occupied about two hectares with two new 22-bed general wards, one for men the other for women, plus separate single wards for observation.

The south facing children's ward had opening doors to a paved terrace allowing cots to be wheeled out. Fourteen beds were planned.

A private pay ward at the rear of the building was also designed as a separate pavilion with an enclosed garden. When complete, the hospital had a capacity of 72 patients.

## Movies ban on bad boys

MAGISTRATES ordered two 12-year-old boys to stay away from the cinema while they served two years probation.

They had admitted smashing the plate-glass window of the Gun Shop, Westgate, and stealing three revolvers and an air pistol worth £2.60.

They smashed the window after failing with a glass-cutter.

They took two six-chamber revolvers, a small revolver and an airgun.

## Lightning ascent

MODERN three-metre ladders were used for the first time to replace a lightning conductor on St Wulfram's Church spire.

The ladders, secured into the spire by iron hooks, run from the top of the tower to the vane at the top of the 48m spire.

Previously, workmen had to scale up the crockets and use kites to lift their equipment.

The old conductor was installed in 1860.

## Jilted man stole hat

A 25-year-old from Union Street, recently an inmate at the Poor Law institution, was sent to jail for a month after stealing a hat worth 29.5p plus 18.5p cash from his landlord.

He said: "I met a girl and hoped I would marry but after a row I had with her mother she wouldn't see me again. I was so upset I didn't know what to do so I committed this offence."

# 1934     Grantham in the News

## Sounding different

THE pronunciation of the town's name was changing, according to Oxford University Press tome The Sounds of Standard English by J. Nicklin MA.

It said: "the termination –ham has suffered developments.

"Although we may still hear Grant-m or perhaps better Grahnt-m, the pronunciation Gran-tham is becoming more and more common".

He said this was quite common with English names

## Fewer drunks as police step up visits to pubs

A MEETING of Grantham Brewster Sessions was told there were a total of 84 licensed premises in the borough.

Forty-nine of these were fully licensed houses with 25 beer houses, two off-licences and eight wine merchants.

There were also eight registered clubs and a theatre bar.

A police spokesman said all of the premises were visited a total of 308 times during the year and were satisfied that most of them were well conducted.

Seven cases of drunkenness were reported.

## The lady wows fans

LADY Brownlow was joined by other talented actors to perform A Bill of Divorcement written by Clemence Dane.

The week-long performance was staged at the Theatre Royal, George Street.

The run raised more than £200 for Grantham Hospital.

The audiences, especially among the working classes, were said to be overwhelmed by her ladyship's performances.

## Epidemic spotted

A SERIOUS epidemic of measles broke out in town, especially among the very young.

Emergency precautions were put into effect to curb the spread and several schools closed.

Brownlow Infants School in Finkin Street was shut down for several weeks because of the high number of infections.

## Archbishop

THE Rev J W C Wand, who was born in Manthorpe Road, Grantham, was consecrated Archbishop of Brisbane at St Paul's Cathedral, London.

He had been fellow and dean at Oriel College, Oxford, since 1925.

---

### BABY CARRIAGE

The Latest Designs.

Comfortable Hygienic, Smart.

We are now making a Special Show of the famous "PEDIGREE" PRAMS.
Built like a motor car, well upholstered and super sprung, they are the "Ide Pram. Their ease of running and beautiful finish will be readily appreciated See them now in our Windows, and ask for Special Illustrated Catalogue
Prices from £2/7/6 to £10/10/0.

### WALLPAPERS

Our New 1934 Designs have now arrived, and we have a choice selection on show from 3d per roll. Be sure and see them. Pattern Books on loan.

### G. H. NEALE & SONS, LTD.,
Home Furnishing Specialists,
'Phone 106.     77, WESTGATE, GRANTHAM.
Also Bourne and Sleaford

# Grantham in the News — 1934

## Aveling Barford arrival signals a boom time ahead

GRANTHAM put the recession behind it and was on the road to prosperity.

In 18 months, the dole queue was slashed from 2,300 to just over 1,000. The town was booming thanks mainly to the effort of Coun Stanley Foster.

Leading the revival was Aveling Barford, the road-roller manufacturer which moved from Rochester to a 20-hectare site of former brickworks on Houghton Road.

Once in full production, the company expected to employ 2,000 men.

A further 500 jobs were created at a newly opened tannery, Bjorlow, on Earlesfield Lane.

Maltings which had also been in danger of closure were purchased by Bass Breweries of Burton-on-Trent and returned to full production.

More factories were expected to arrive the following year.

*Union Court, Inner Street being demolished with Ruston and Hornsby in the background.*

## Demolition of slum terraces

WORK began on demolishing unfit houses in Inner Street.

Known as the streets behind the chimneys, they were built hurriedly in the early 19th Century for workers who left the land to work in Richard Hornsby's factory.

But the homes had few conveniences, rising damp and leaky roofs.

Toilets and running water were outside with little chance of moving them inside.

Several families relied on a shared standpipe and privies in the backyard.

There was no electricity, only gas and, in most cases, paraffin lamps was the only artificial lighting.

## It's a lottery to occupy houses on Grantham's newest estate

THE occupiers of the first four houses built on former allotments off Springfield Road was decided by ballot.

They were the first of 100 being built for essential workers at Aveling Barford being transferred from Rochester in Kent.

Mr E Barford, son-in-law of Lord Ashfield, who inspected the new houses, said they were of the best possible design and standard.

The estate was called Walton Gardens after the ancient settlement on the site of which the houses were built.

## Gift to the town

A PAIR of ornamental bronze vases was presented to the borough by Aveling Barford, to mark their transferring to the town from Rochester, Kent.

They were handed over at a formal dinner and were installed outside the ballroom.

The Chinese designed ornaments were three-metres tall and weighed 180kg each.

They were bought 30 years earlier for the company's Rochester offices. Director W G Barford said they would be out of place in the new offices.

## Osiers were pea sticks - man claims

A GRANTLEY Street man was fined 1.5p for damaging an osier bed belonging to Rothwell Lee.

He had cut six bushes of willows with a knife made from an old scythe at the beds near the Grantham Canal. The defendant claimed the osiers in his possession were pea sticks from his own garden.

# 1934 Grantham in the News

## Tight fit

A PAIR of traction engines tow a giant casting made in Lincoln, through Grantham.

The road train managed to squeeze through the ton's narrow streets.

It was captured passing the George Hotel and the newly opened Marks & Spencer store, High Street.

## Time called

ELIZABETH Richardson, landlady of the Anchor, Wide Westgate, died aged 91.

She had been at the pub 63 years.

Up to her death she was England's oldest owner-innkeeper.

## Get digging jobless told

UNEMPLOYED men were told to take up working allotments.

George Giles, of the National Allotments Association, told a meeting at the Cambridge Street Rooms, that as well as self sufficiency, they could learn a new trade.

He said: "They could earn a livelihood as poultry keepers, market gardeners or pig farmers."

From left: Ald Theo Rawle, Dr. C H D Robbs, Mr T H Edwards, Christopher H Turnor, Ald H Beeden, Sir Charles Welby, W T Phipps, Coun F Read, Rev H E Stancliffe, Ald F Weekley (Mayor), Mr A R Bellamy, Mr W. Rowell, The Rev G H Warde (Vicar of Grantham) and headteacher Mr C. Bispham.

## King's opens engineering workshop

THE latest development at the King's School was an engineering workshop, opened by Ruston and Hornsby director R A Bellamy.

It was equipped with modern tools by both his company and new town firm Aveling Barford.

Master in charge Mr E Elms said the new workshop was not to prepare pupils to become tradesmen but to help them to understand industry and broaden their interests.

Headteacher Mr Bispham said it was the first new building at the school since 1904.

He said: "This will give boys contacts with ordinary life so they can leave school with an interest already awakened.

"The man must rule the machine, not the machine rule the man."

# Grantham in the News  1934

## Grantham reaps whirlwind

TWO footballers were struck by lightning, market stalls were overturned and a greenhouse roof was hurled 60 metres in a whirlwind that carved a path of destruction through Grantham

It struck at 4.30pm on a Saturday dominated by black clouds and heavy rains.

Following a crack of thunder, T Nichols, of Mowbrays FC, and a Cranwell aircraftman were hurled to the ground by a lightning strike on Dysart Road as they played football.

Both recovered after only a few days.

The roof of a greenhouse was blown away from Harlaxton Road allotments, near the gasworks, and tiles were blown from roofs in the area.

Coats outside High Street outfitters Sheppard's were blown away and a market stall upskittled as whirlwind moved on the town centre.

It was all over in minutes.

## Bishop's son in mountain tragedy

PAUL Wand, the son of Grantham-born Archbishop of Brisbane, Australia, Dr J W C Wand, was found dead in a crevasse near Mont Blanc.

His body was discovered with fellow climber John Hoyland.

The undergraduates are believed to have fallen about 700m.

Their bodies were found by Frank Smythe, a member of the 1933 Everest expedition.

## Island fling

THE Town Council called on the Ministry of Transport to improve road safety at the London Road-Bridge End Road junction.

They said for the safety of pedestrians, refuge islands must be installed at the junction on all four roads.

## New development will turn Earlesfield into a small town

THE most ambitious housing scheme for many years was launched by Long Eaton architect E Hooley.

He bought 16 hectares of land opposite the workhouse on Dysart Road to develop housing which he planned to rent at between 55p and 67p per week.

The first tenants moved in just before Christmas.

The owner also offered a hectare of land for use as a children's playground.

A spokesman said that once complete, the Earlesfield area would begin to look like a small town.

Mr Hooley said he planned to name the roads of the new estate after towns on the Isle of Wight.

## Corporate soccer

GRANTHAM Town FC, struggling with financial difficulties, formed a public company to control its affairs.

A meeting at Westgate Hall was told the town's senior football club could not survive unless a closer control on cash was instigated.

A spokesman said: "We would have been unable to continue the way we were. There is no alternative."

*Parking problems on St Peter's Hill*

## Survey to probe traffic

BOROUGH councillors called for a survey to look at the town's parking and road traffic problems.

Many said councillors failed to cater for the growing car-owning population.

The study looked at improving the roads and providing better parking facilities.

# 1935 Grantham in the News

## Private wards are opened at Grantham Hospital

PRIVATE wards built as part of the Grantham Hospital extensions were finished in July.

The six wards had a kitchen. A sisters' room and a room for a private nurse were built at the end of the corridor.

The charge for each room was set at 75p per day or a subscription of £2.10 per year.

Pay beds were also available in the children's ward at £3.15 per week. Medical fees were extra and by arrangement between the patient and doctor.

Chairman of the hospital board, Lord Brownlow, said: "We shall have a hospital which for its size will be second to none in this county."

## Smoking chimney led to discovery

A CHANCE probe into the cause of a smoking chimney led to the discovered of a Tudor fireplace at the King's School.

It was in the nursery of the headmaster's house and was said to be of great significance.

Headmaster Mr Bispham had complained the fireplace in there was useless and the room was unusable in winter.

But when later brickwork was removed the original stonework was found.

## Chief reporter killed by train

GRANTHAM Journal chief reporter Frank Gregory was killed by a train on the foot-crossing near Spittlegate bridge.

He had worked for the newspaper for 37 years.

An inquest was told Mr Gregory (53) had been ill for several weeks, with head pains and was unable to sleep.

He was also distressed by having to give evidence at the Assizes and was upset by changes at the Journal.

Because of these, it was understood he was suffering from loss of confidence.

The coroner recorded that Mr Gregory committed suicide.

## Gas supply switched off in Billingborough

BILLINGBOROUGH Gasworks, established in 1864, closed down due to heavy losses.

The works had been sold in 1920 as a going concern after Billingborough and Horbling Gas Co went bust.

The company tried to continue but electricity finally signalled the death of the smaller gas companies.

Many villagers said they would move to the Mid Lincolnshire Electric Supply Company for their lighting and cooking.

Others said they would much sooner return to oil lamps.

## New Town captain

HARRY Swaby was appointed captain of Grantham Town Football Club.

A former First Division player with Grimsby Town, he was signed from Scarborough.

The move allowed last year's captain, Harry Pringle, to concentrate on his role as manager.

---

**It costs no more to buy the *best* BREAD**

The best of anything usually costs more— but it's different with Bread. All Bread costs the same, so that it pays you more than ever to buy the best—the bread we bake. Try a loaf to-morrow. You will appreciate the difference.

**PARKER & SONS**
GREAT GONERBY

# Grantham in the News — 1935

## Approved school for boy in pink

A WOMAN attendant at Wyndham Park swimming pool who hung her pink bathing costume out to dry was surprised to see it being worn by a young boy.

And when she approached him, the boy, who was on probation, claimed he had bought it from his brother for a halfpenny.

Constance Letts told Grantham juvenile court if he couldn't afford a bathing costume she would have given him one.

Clerk of the Court Aubrey Malin said: "Boys who are on probation get a good deal more than those who are not."

After being ordered to plead guilty to the theft, the youngster was sent to an approved school for three years.

## Profit rising

GRANTHAM and Lincoln engineers Ruston and Hornsby showed £88,277 profit compared with £55,224 the previous year.

But directors warned the outlook was bleak as Europe was an increasingly difficult market.

## Saw finger

STEPHEN Lambert, a sawyer, lost a finger while working at Spittlegate Ironworks.

A plank on the mechanical saw he was operating slipped, throwing his hand against the blade.

Mr Lambert, of Dysart Road, an officer at Wharf Road Baptist Church, also seriously injured another finger

*Award-winning Paradise Place*

## Blaze of colour for town's civic celebrations

THE streets were a blaze of colour as Grantham celebrated Civic Week in June.

The Mayor and Mayoress, Lord and Lady Brownlow, toured the town with the tough task of picking the best decorated streets.

Best short street prize went to Paradise Place, which had only 11 households. Of those, nine heads of the households were either unemployed or widowed.

The Brownlows invited them all to a strawberry tea at Belton Park. Second was Vere Court. Inner Street was the pick of the larger streets with New Street second.

The civic parade was a washout. A violent storm drenched the marchers and kept the crowds away. The highlight was the Pageant of Youth in Wyndham Park, performed by 2,000 local children and watched by 10,000 adults.

## Special award for brave farmer's son

A HOUGHAM youth, recovering from a bad chill, ignored personal risk by leaping into the swollen River Witham to try and save a drowning boy.

Although seven-year-old Norman Webb died, heroic farmer's son William Hickson (18) was awarded a vellum certificate by the Royal Humane Society.

William spotted the youngster paddling in the river near his home but the boy slipped near the sluice.

He was carried by the strong current into four metres of water. William jumped in after him but failed to save his life.

## General reception

GENERAL Evangeline Booth, Supreme Commander of the Salvation Army, stopped at Grantham during her 1,600km motorcade.

The gathering was held at the London Road football ground on a wet Monday.

# 1935 Grantham in the News

## Farmer killed by cow

ALLINGTON farmer Arthur Wing (66) died after being kicked by a cow.

He was separating it from its calf when it lashed out hitting him in the stomach.

Dr Jocelyn Jauch told an inquest that Mr Wing died in Grantham Hospital of peritonitis resulting from a ruptured bowel.

## Going loco

LNER announced plans for major improvements to Grantham locomotive depot.

Sixty-four engines would be stationed in Grantham, using 1,000 tonnes of coal weekly.

Two engine pits, one 50m long and the other 30m long were built, each one metre deep.

## House fire

BLACK House Farm, behind the King's School playing field was gutted by fire, leaving only four charred walls.

## Post Offices opened

TWO new sub-post offices opened in February, one on Dysart Road, run by Mr S Foster, the other on Springfield Road, run by Miss E Hutchinson.

## Two pubs close

TWO inns, the Shepherd and Dog, Wide Westgate, and the Blue Boat, Old Wharf, were declared redundant by Spittlegate licensing justices.

Brewers Mowbray claimed £1,554 and £944 in compensation respectively.

## Sailor stops express train

THE Grantham driver and fireman of the King's Cross to Glasgow train had quite a shock when a sailor appeared from the coal tender while the train was travelling at 60mph through Huntingdonshire.

Driver G Mills, of Huntingtower Road, and fireman W. Christian, were preparing to defend his cab with a shovel when the sailor explained he was on a mercy mission.

He had broken through the locked door to inform the driver his companion was unconscious in one of the compartments.

His colleague George Brown had been struck by four mailbags while looking out of the window.

He said he had pulled the communication cord but it did not respond.

Other passengers had pulled him back when he attempted to edge along the footboard to the engine.

The locomotive pulled up at Peterborough where Mr Brown was taken to hospital.

### Lucky escape

SIX-year-old Edmund Chamberlain had a lucky escape when he was impaled on a spiked iron fence.

Edmund, of Agnes Terrace, East Street, was on the wall which bounded his street from the River Witham, when he slipped.

A spike on the wall pierced his throat. He returned to school a few days later.

## Modest hero is rewarded

AN RAF corporal, stationed at Grantham, was presented with the Royal Humane Society's testimonial after jumping into a river to rescue a small boy.

He then recovered his jacket and walked away.

It happened on the River Ouse, York, when Walter Martin was visiting his parents.

After the rescue, he handed Charles Butler (4) to his parents and walked away.

---

A FREE BOND STREET TREATMENT

Jane Seymour expert at
**Whysall & Son's.**
* Note the dates - FEB. 18 TO FEB. 23

Jane Seymour's expert will be in attendance for one week only. She will do, completely free of charge, facial treatment exactly as it is practised in her Salons in Bond Street. Learn how to give yourself more effective treatment in your own home.

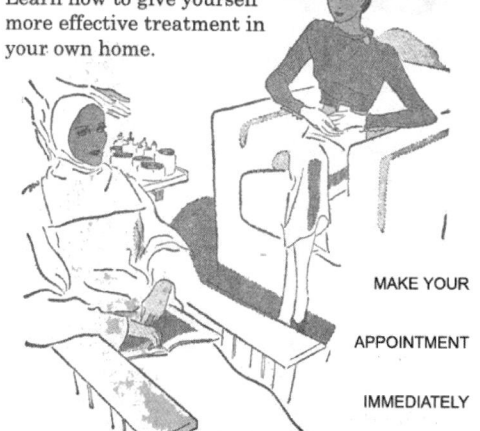

MAKE YOUR APPOINTMENT IMMEDIATELY

**WHYSALL & SON,**
Toilet Specialists,
GRANTHAM.

# Grantham in the News — 1935

## 'Fagin' mum sent to jail

A MAN interrupted proceedings at Grantham magistrates court after his wife and daughter were sentenced for theft.

He called out: "When she comes out I will be dead and I shall lose my job. I have lost my wife and I shall lose my child."

It followed the theft of a woman's handbag at Grantham market.

Witnesses said the mother nodded towards the girl who immediately snatched the handbag containing 80p from a shopper's basket.

The woman then shouted: "Go on, run."

After being sentenced to one month in prison, the woman struggled violently with police and said: "God help the one who sent me."

The girl was sent to an industrial school for three years.

Her father then collapsed and had to be revived in an ante room.

## Council rejects plans to provide pensions for all employees

KESTEVEN County Council decided to introduce a superannuation scheme for its clerical staff - but there wasn't a scheme for manual workers.

Councillors said they could afford it for higher paid staff but not for those referred to as 'bottom dogs' such as roadmen.

Ald George Jenkinson told councillors: "There are 120 men employed on roads.

"It's all right being generous, but whose money are you being generous with?

" The ratepayers of course."

## New hall for St John's Church

A MODEL of the proposed St John's Church Hall, Launder Terrace, was commissioned by the church.

The original intention had been to build a large hall in the vicarage garden, fronting Station Road East.

But when the church had the opportunity to buy Home House, former residence of the Coultas family, for £300, they jumped at the chance.

A flat-roof extension would be built behind in Queen Street costing a further £900.

It was planned to raise funds by selling specially made bricks to be used in the extension.

Each brick was to bear the buyer's name.

## Two die in lorry crash

TWO lorry drivers died following a head-on collision at Haceby Hollow, near Ropsley.

George Hawes, of Norwich, died at the scene and Harold Lyons (32), of St Helens, died of injuries in Grantham Hospital.

An inquest was told Mr Lyons was in good health and previously had an accident-free record.

Several others remained injured in hospital.

They were treated at the scene by Folkingham GP Dr Stanton.

# 1935 Grantham in the News

## Farmer survives bull attack

FARMER H R Owen, of Bridge End had a lucky escape when he was gored and tossed by a bull.

Only the intervention of neighbour A J Allen saved him from certain death.

Mr Owen, chairman of Horbling parish council, was crossing the field to feed his chickens when the bull attacked.

He held on to its horns but became exhausted and lost consciousness.

Mr Allen, who was on his way to Hoffleet Stow was attracted by the behaviour of other beast.

He then saw the bull turn a man over with his head. He grabbed two pitchforks and with the aid of shepherd Mr Pearson and his sheepdog forced the bull to run away.

Dr Morris, of Donington, said no bones were broken but Mr Owen suffered severe bruising and lacerations.

## Lorry runs into front room

A PENSIONER had a lucky escape when a lorry carrying six tonnes of machinery crashed through the front of his Gonerby Hill Foot house.

Fred Hackney had just left the front room when the lorry driven by Roy Harris, of Hull, slipped out of gear on Gonerby Hill.

Harris was fined £2 for having inefficient brakes.

## It's safety first for Grantham

GRANTHAM was the safest town in Britain to cross the road.

The Ministry of Transport said in 1935, not one death was caused through a road accident, the only place in Britain with a 20,000-plus population to achieve this.

This was despite the busy A1 Great North Road running through the town centre.

## Pilot dies in air crash

ACTING Pilot Officer Robert Abercromby Yale (22) was killed when his Tutor aeroplane crashed near Wood Nook, less than a mile from Grantham Aerodrome where he was based.

Villager William Tempest said he saw the plane nosedive straight into a pea field. It did not catch fire.

Experts from the RAF said the aeroplane appeared to turn too steeply and the pilot lost control.

An inquest was told Mr Yale was not an experienced pilot and as a pupil would not naturally go into a dive. His parachute had been released from the pack but was not used.

The coroner recorded death by misadventure.

### St John's field a fine performance

MEMBERS of St John Amateur Dramatic Society put on a performance of The Lilies of the Field. It was staged at the YMCA, Wharf Road.

## Tax rise is not harmful to us says director

A DIRECTOR of Ruston and Hornsby said the increased tax on heavy oils should not hit the manufacture of diesel engines.

Commenting on the just under 1p per litre increase on tax, Mr A R Bellamy said: "This type of engine is still more economical than the petrol engine.

"I cannot see the extra tax halting our development work.

"We shall be all the more keen to improve it still further to show it has economies outside the mere price of fuel."

# Grantham in the News — 1935

## Sparrows blamed for house fires

TWO sparrows were blamed for a fire which left two families homeless and three houses badly damaged.

It began in Mr Singleton's house in Edward Street, where he lived with his invalid wife and son. It then spread to other properties.

He said: "Two sparrows built their nest over the bathroom at the rear of the house, through a broken bar in the grating."

One day Mr Singleton decided to fix the gap with zinc but not having a long enough ladder, decided to smoke them out but this was unsuccessful.

He said: "I couldn't get enough smoke so I gave up and went to work.

"Unfortunately, the fire I lit in the bathroom was not fully extinguished and it spread."

Firefighters took an hour to bring the blaze under control although they caused as much damage as the blaze.

**Millard's Place, Vere Court**

## Condemned homes could be made fit again says landlord

A PROPERTY owner claimed homes the council condemned to be pulled down, could be improved instead.

Medical officer Dr C H D Robbs had claimed the homes in Millard's Place, Vere Court, should be razed to the ground.

He said they were all unfit for human habitation because of poor natural lighting, low bulging roofs, defective brickwork, bulging walls and little ventilation.

He said it was a disgrace that 121 people were forced to live in them.

But Mr Barnes, on behalf of the Thomas Millard estate, said the houses could be renovated. He said a tremendous amount of money had already been spent on them.

Town clerk Aubrey Malim said it was best to pull them down and move the tenants to new homes in Harrowby.

## Bookmaking brothers were not on a good bet says court

TWO brothers were fined £10 each for running a betting business in a wooden shed behind 20 Oxford Street.

Police, who raided the building, said they found Raymond Measures, marking up the day's runners from a racing newspaper. His brother Edward was also there.

A Crown and Anchor board, used for gambling, was also found.

Borough magistrates were told up to 41 men had been seen in the building.

The chairman said: "This kind of practice must be stamped out."

## Canal concerns

ALDERMAN Forsgate Weekeley saud the Grantham Canal could become derelict unless it got urgent attention.

He said owners Great Northern Railway wanted nothing more to do with it and its only use in future would be as a drainage source.

He added that unless something was done, it could even become a cause of flooding in the Harlaxton Road area.

# Grantham in the News  1936

## Mining will leave village desolate - claim

PLANS to close footpaths to allow iron ore mining around Colsterworth were condemned by a rural councillor.

Ald Simmonds said in 20 years when the ironstone company had finished its workings, there would be left a desolate spot.

But his plea fell on deaf eyes. The committee agreed to the closures by 22 votes to two on condition that Frodingham Ironstone Company would build a road from Water Lane.

Mr Simmonds said: "Not so long ago we had 200 pilgrims come to Woolsthorpe Manor.

"Now they could only look on this area with dismay."

## Plans to build new store

THE building at the top of St Catherine's Road was due to be replaced by the new Co-op store.

Work began the following year.

## Drunk woman tore police blankets

A FORTY-nine-year-old woman of no fixed address was sentenced to a month's hard labour after being found guilty of being drunk and disorderly and causing wilful damage.

She was arrested by two constables, called to the Black Dog, Watergate, by the landlady Mrs Steele.

Pc Bell told borough magistrates: "She began to sing disgusting songs and interfered with passers-by.

"She made an obscene expression and laid on her back in the road."

She was taken to the police station in a taxi where she fought with officers.

Kelly ripped up the police report and tore blankets worth 80p in her cell.

She told magistrates her behaviour was due to being "mad through starvation".

## Lightning strike woman rescued

A WOMAN was buried by masonry when lightning struck her Horbling Fen home.

Mrs Rollins, who lived with her husband and seven children, was returning to her kitchen in a storm when a bolt of lightning struck the chimney stack. In seconds she was buried by bricks and mortar.

Fortunately, she was spotted by farm foreman Mr Thurman who dug through the debris to rescue her.

She was treated for head and facial cuts and bruises.

Tiles also crashed from the roof, leaving furniture and bedding exposed to the storm. A baby asleep in the kitchen was unharmed.

## New pub

A NEW public house, the Three Gables, on Gorse Rise, was approved by Grantham licensing sessions.

The pub took over the licence of the Crown and Anchor, Swinegate, on condition owners Mowbray's, whose London Road brewery also surrendered the licence of the Musicians' Arms, Wharf Road.

## Bells rehung at village church

THE bells of Skillington parish church were renovated at a cost of £200. Rehanging them took about two weeks.

They were dedicated by the vicar, the Rev H C Cane.

# Grantham in the News — 1936

## Garage man burned as petrol ignites

ARTHUR Simmonds, of the Ermine Cafe, Colsterworth, was badly burned when he helped a passing motorist.

He had locked up for the night when he was flagged down by a driver who had nearly run out of petrol.

Mr Simmonds put down his hurricane lamp near the petrol pump and inserted the nozzle into the driver's tank.

The nozzle dropped out and fell on the lamp, which burst into flames.

Mr Simmonds was engulfed in flames but fortunately was wearing leather leggings which probably saved his life.

The flames were beaten out using an old mackintosh.

He was taken to Dr Mitchell's surgery by a passing motorist.

He said afterwards in future he will use a flashlight when serving petrol at night.

*The new lorries lined up in Wide Westgate*

## Gold letter day for brewery

MOWBRAY'S Brewery took delivery of nine Bedford lorries worth £3,500.

They were supplied by Whipples, of Watergate.

Managing director Fred Whipple formally handed them over to the brewery's manager Mr W H B Howell, in Wide Westgate.

The blue and gold livery was by signwriters Cope and Son, of Wharf Road. Each truck had 155 letters in 23-carat gold leaf.

## New industry for Grantham

SULLIVAN Machinery Co, one of the leading manufacturers of coal cutting machinery, took over a surplus workshop at Ruston and Hornsby, London Road.

After moving its works from Letchworth, it called its part of the factory Grange Works.

A company spokesman said Grantham's position on the Great North Road and main railway line was the deciding factor.

## Drivers in lucky escape

TWO Glasgow men had a lucky escape when their pantechnicon furniture lorry ploughed into a London Road shop owned by electrical engineer P Baxter.

The strength of the cab and the Triplex glass was said to be the reason they suffered only from shock as bricks and broken glass flew everywhere.

The shop, complete with its contents of wireless equipment and baby linen, was destroyed.

During a heavy snowstorm, the lorry had collided with a traffic island which it destroyed, before crashing into the shop.

Furniture inside the vehicle, including a piano, was badly damaged.

## Blow for church

A GALE blew a pinnacle off the roof of All Saints' Church, Hough-on-the-Hill, tearing a huge hole in the roof.

After displacing an oak beam in the roof, the stone hit the ground, shattering into three pieces.

## Woman's car was moved twice

MRS Beatrice Maskell-Hall of Norman Leys, Beacon Lane, Grantham, was fined £1 at Grantham police court for obstructing High Street with her car.

Pc Albert Beecroft told magistrates he had made a note of all parked cars at 11am and 15 minutes later all but Mrs Maskell-Hall's had moved on.

Twice he allowed lorry drivers to move the vehicle so they could make deliveries before she finally returned at noon.

# 1936 Grantham in the News

## Eerie time at village inn

MYSTERY tappings, eerie footsteps and nocturnal knockings disturbed people at a village inn.

The deep shadows in the passageways of the Fighting Cocks, Corby, and bolted doors found open, often struck terror in human hearts.

Strange noises were also being heard at the hostelry.

Licensees Mr and Mrs Atkins said fear had forced them to leave the pub and stay with friends on several occasions.

## Lorry was not fit for the road

A LORRY driver and its owner, both from Leeds, were summoned by Grantham magistrates over a vehicle not fit for the road.

It was said to be a danger to other road users.

Vehicle examiner John Brown said the sides of the lorry were tied with string, nails were used instead of fastenings, the petrol cap was missing, the shackle springs loose and the steering in poor condition.

The owner was fined £5 and the driver 50p.

## Retirement for body hand cart

IN future, bodies of suicides and accidental deaths would be conveyed to the mortuary in a motorised hearse replacing the hand-bier.

Each body would also be placed in a zinc-lined elm coffin, cleaned out regularly for re-use.

Welcoming the Borough Council's change of mind, Coun Mrs Barnes said: "I'm very pleased. The old practice was an eyesore."

Ald Rothell Lee said the new arrangement would cost 50p per removal.

## Deserted Australian sleeping rough

LABOURER Thomas Healer was sentenced to one month's hard labour after being found guilty of sleeping out without means of subsistence.

Pc Bramhall found him in a house in Middlemore Yard, Castlegate, which was being demolished. There was neither roof nor stairs in the building.

When the constable awoke him, Healey asked: "Where else can I go?"

Healey came from Australia but instead of returning, he married an Englishwoman who had since deserted him.

Grantham Borough Court heard he received £1.50 per week from a job with the corporation and said he had no need to sleep rough.

## Overtime saves property

AN employer working late at architects Traylen and Lenton alerted firefighters after smelling smoke from neighbouring offices, Kesteven Insurance Company, on the coner of Finkin Street and High Street.

It was discovered that joists over a fireplace were smouldering and had to be removed.

Stationers J P Nightingale, which occupied the shop below, suffered damaged mainly from smoke and debris.

---

**HALFORD'S FOR RALEIGH**

See the Range of Raleigh Cycles at your Halford Depot

**THE GOLDEN ARROW MODEL. £5 · 19 · 6**
*Easy Payments arranged*

This is the famous model so widely advertised - the speedman's ideal. See the Golden Arrow "in the steel" at your local Halford Depot - handle it. Remember, a bicycle bought from Halford's enjoys free after-sales service from every Depot throughout the country. In your Halford Depot you will see bicycles and everything for the machine and rider; camping equipment, tools, accessories and kit for tourists, and they are all listed in the Halford Catalogue. If you like the open road you will like this book. It is free and post free. Write for it today.

THE HALFORD CYCLE CO. LTD.

Local Branch

**6 Watergate GRANTHAM**

# Grantham in the News — 1936

## Eight killed as trains collide

FIVE men were killed and three died from horrific injuries in a railway crash at Barkston.

Four others were left fighting for their lives in Grantham Hospital.

They were in the brake van of a ballast train, going to platelaying work at Newark. Two light engines coupled together ploughed into it.

The driver of one of the York-bound locomotives was unaware of the incident, as the van they hit disintegrated like matchwood.

Dr Jocelyn Jauch and Dr James Hopper drove to the scene to help the victims.

Hundreds of volunteer railwaymen and their families turned up to help with the rescue.

Driver, David Ward, acting fireman Harold Calvert and George Smith who drove the other engine were charged with manslaughter but acquitted at Lincoln Assizes.

## Soaked Old Boys stage a walk out

SOAKING players called a halt to the Grantham League match between Aveling Barford (the 'Rollers') and Spitalgate Old Boys, played in sleet and snow on the Houghton Road ground.

At half time, with Old Boys trailing 4-0, drenched players asked the Rollers' captain Ayres to abandon the match, but he refused.

They reluctantly returned to the field of play but 15 minutes from time all but four of them staged a walk-off.

The referee was forced to stop the match with the score at 7-0.

## Pilots die in mid-air crash

TWO pilots were killed in a mid-air collision between two Grantham-based planes over Easton.

One of them, former Etonian, Acting Flying Officer Geoffrey King George (21) died after leaping from his plane by parachute and landing in a tree.

Leading Aircraftman P J Pugh died in the collision.

## Disabled man drowns in wheelchair fall

NORMAN Kirkby (26), of the County Institution, Hill View, Dysart Road, was found dead after telling a fellow inmate "I'm going out tomorrow".

He drowned in a disused quarry after plunging eight metres in his wheelchair.

His mother, Amy Gertrude Kirkby, of Edward Street, said her son was crippled from the waist down. His arms were also weak.

She said he had been in the institution for about nine years.

She said: "He was too heavy for me to look after and was depressed. I have two other little ones."

William Wilkinson said Mrs Kirkby told him he was leaving the following day.

Sergeant Curry said the chair had not run away but had been propelled towards the edge of the disused quarry.

Recording a verdict of suicide while in unsound mind coroner Aubrey Malim said: "There is little doubt it was not an accident."

## Extra time for boozers

GRANTHAM'S drinkers got a special summer treat from magistrates although their opposite numbers in Spittlegate were disappointed.

Grantham licensing sessions agreed to extend closing time from 10pm to 10.30pm from May to September. In winter, licensing hours remained at 6pm to 10pm.

Spittlegate Magistrates meanwhile, decided to keep things as they were.

# 1936 Grantham in the News

## Gypsy's final wish

THE deathbed wish of Everard 'Ebb' Smith (60), chief of the gypsies camped at Waltham-on-the-Wolds, was carried out.

After morning service, the eldest son set fire to his father's £500 caravan.

Ebb's widow and eight children watched for an hour until his possessions were destroyed by the flames.

## Drop in jobless

UNEMPLOYMENT in Grantham fell below 800 for the first time in seven years.

The May figure of 757 was the lowest since November 1929. It topped 2,340 in January 1933. It was a drop of 99 from the previous month and 375 less than the previous year.

Grantham's jobless was made up of 645 men, 16 boys, 73 women and 23 girls.

Colsterworth had 117 out of work compared with 157 in 1935.

## Labour home

GRANTHAM Labour Party opened its first permanent headquarters in premises opposite the Westgate Hall.

## Estate road named

THE principal road of the new Cherry Orchard estate built off New Beacon Road was to be called Beeden Grove after Ald Harry Beeden. It was later changed to Uplands Drive.

Other roads would be Belmont Grove, Ermine Close and Central Place.

## Kiddies were forced to burgle vacant house

A NINETEEN-year-old youth from Charles Street, Grantham, acted like Fagin in Dickens' Oliver Twist.

He was sent to jail for a month after Grantham police court heard how he twisted the arms of younger boys if they refused to work for him.

He sent them into empty houses to open the doors for him.

The offences came to light when a gas meter reader went to three empty houses in South Parade and another in Hand's Yard.

He said the meters had been broken into and 40p stolen altogether. Damage caused was £1.88.

A 10-year-old told the court, the youth said he would twist the arms of both him and his friend if they refused to help him.

They were discovered by the younger boy's mother after she demanded to know how he could afford to visit the Picture House.

When he told her, she gave him a good hiding, sent him to bed and called the police.

The Youth pleaded guilty and told the court he was sorry.

## Courting to blame

GEORGE Patman, of Dysart Road, Grantham, was fined 25p for allowing two horses to stray on to Harlaxton Road.

He told Spittlegate magistrates: "The gate must have been left open by courting couples who frequently use this field."

## New life

FIFTY-seven families, mainly from heavy industry and coal mines in County Durham, moved to Harrowby to become market gardeners.

They were the new members of the Land Settlement Association which gave men displaced from the heavy industries a chance to live and work in the countryside.

About 59 smallholdings were created near Harrowby Hall with a central marketing structure.

### SAY "99"

You may not know but we have a fully equipped and competent Service Department which specialises in Radio Repairs. This department has its own technical staff and is always ready to help you if your set needs a "tonic".
If you are having any troubles just let us examine the set and we will quote you at once - none of this servicing first and sending you a large bill afterwards. We believe in giving our customers a straight deal - shouldn't be Murphy Dealers if we didn't.

Murphy Sets from £6 7s 6d to £14 10s 0d.

ALL MODELS AVAILABLE FOR A.C. OR D.C. MAINS. HIRE PURCHASE TERMS ON ALL MODELS

### BURGESS & COULSON
40 WATERGATE   TEL. 395

THE
**ONLY MURPHY DEALER IN GRANTHAM**

# Grantham in the News — 1936

## Youth dies in pit used as medical cure

A FIFTEEN-year-old boy died after falling into a pit containing ammonia and other tar by-products at Grantham Gasworks, where he was employed.

Eric Cook fell because the covering had been removed, to allow local children to inhale the fumes as a method of curing whooping cough.

Grantham Coroner A C Malim said no blame was attached to anyone, although he praised two fellow employees who went to his rescue.

Henry Hutchins, of New Street, put on a respirator and went into the pit but failed to find him.

Eric, of Norton Street, had been employed at the gasworks for about a year.

Mrs Wright, of Brook Street, had taken her child to breathe the fumes, when she saw a young man disappear into the hole. His hands were outstretched.

Dr C H D Robbs said death was due to drowning.

Factory inspector Miss V Chinn said there should be a one-metre high fence around any holes in a chemical factory.

She said: "No doubt it will be done in future. That is as far as I will go." The coroner returned a verdict of accidental death.

## Peregrine is King's stand-in

KING Edward VIII was godparent to Edward John Peregrine Cust, who was christened in the private chapel of his Belton House home.

The King was unable to attend the ceremony so the boy's father, Lord Brownlow, stood proxy.

*Police line up outside the Public Library*

## Police train for gas warfare

POLICE in Grantham attended lectures and took part in demonstrations on wearing protective clothing against gas warfare.

They were fully protected and used teargas for the demonstration. They also used a special Home Office van for their training.

Sergeant Todd from county headquarters, who was in charge, said: "Every part of the body must be protected in the case of a mustard gas attack."

## Police catch motorist in high-speed chase

POLICE chased a car at speeds of up to 50mph in the early hours of the morning.

Sgt Humberstone was on patrol when he spotted the car without lights at Corby Glen.

As he approached, the vehicle shot off so he set off in pursuit in his own car.

He chased the vehicle, driven by William Wells, of Nottingham, through Boothby Pagnell and along the road to Great Ponton.

The sergeant told Spttilegate magistrates that game was being tossed out of Wells' car window as it drove along.

The chase ended when the car skidded 25metres after taking a corner at 30mph, hitting a kerb and damaging the wheels.

Wells was fined £4 and his licence suspended for a month for dangerous driving.

# 1937     Grantham in the News

## Villagers opposed to having mains water

WEST Kesteven Council's plans to put 12 villages on to mains water ran into opposition from residents.

Honington and Caythorpe representatives said they already had adequate supplies and didn't want the upheaval.

But others welcomed the £30,900 scheme.

Hougham's clerk said people living in the main street had to fetch water from a nearby farmstead or the iron pump in Manor Lane.

He said: "In dry times the wells are filled by the River Witham after flowing up the parish sewer."

Other villages were Allington, Barkston, Carlton Scroop, Foston, Marston, Normanton, Syston, Westborough and Dry Doddington.

## Farmers had a ball

A RECORD 503 tickets were sold for the farmers' ball on New Year's Eve.

The ball, held in the Guildhall ballroom, was an immense success with Billy Merrin and his Commanders.

## Farmer forgot to pick up his trailer

FARMER William Horace Brownlow, of Casthorpe, was fined 25p for leaving his trailer without lights in Westgate overnight.

Mr Brownlow, chairman of the Grantham branch of the National Farmers Union, disconnected the trailer from his car when he went to hospital to collect an injured workman.

He told Grantham borough court: "I parked the trailer because it didn't seem nice to leave it outside the hospital.

"Unfortunately, I then forgot all about it."

## Cat for violent robbers

TWO South Witham men each received 18 strokes of the cat and six month's imprisonment for robbery with violence.

They admitted stealing an attaché case containing £40 from Ada Starsmore, of Stamford.

As she left her home for work at a coal merchants in the town, the two men struck her from behind and she suffered several blows before letting go of the case.

Mr Justice Swift told Birmingham Assizes: "I think it would be good for everybody if you feel some of the pain you inflicted on this girl.

"I have no sympathy for you."

## Protestor at the Manor

THREATS to demolish the 90-year-old Harlaxton Manor were lifted when it was bought by capital punishment opponent Mrs Violet Van der Elst.

The estate was sold three weeks earlier at auction in 100 lots for £20,000.

It had been bought by Mr E Marshall, of Nottingham, a descendant of Gregory Gregory who built it. Mr Marshall sold off the timber for £16,100.

He had planned to demolish the stately home if no buyer could be found.

Mrs Van der Elst bought not only the house but 427 acres of parkland including three lakes.

---

**SPRING CLEANING**
Now is the time to Renew those Old Floor Coverings
CALL and SEE our NEW STOCKS of all the LATEST DESIGNS in CARPETS and LINOS, Etc.

Special Range of CARPET SQUARES in Axminster and Wilton and Tapestry at Keen Prices
STAIR CARPETS of every description.

LINOS from 3/9 per square yard 2 yards wide

Barfelt and Lancastream FLOOR COVERING from 1/11 yard, 2 yards wide

SPECIAL SHOW of CARPETS and LINOS now on show in OUR WINDOWS
SEE US ABOUT YOUR REPAIRS and RENOVATIONS.
EVERYTHING FOR THE HOME AT

**G. H. NEALE & Sons, Ltd.**
Complete House Furnishers
ATLAS HOUSE
77 WESTGATE    Phone 106    GRANTHAM

# Grantham in the News — 1937

## Councillors grapple with all-in wrestling problem

COUN Alfred Roberts struck a blow for public morals when he condemned the council for allowing all-in wrestling at the Westgate Hall.

He said: "This brutal and barbaric pastime is at variance with the council's wish to uplift people both in body and mind.

"I cannot understand anyone with a decent mind indulging in watching such a pastime."

More than 500 people turned up at the protest meeting organised by cross-denominational group The Grantham Brotherhood.

Promoter Mr Johanfesson told them: "Come into the ring and explain to the crowd why there should be no wrestling in town."

The following week Mr Johanfesson said he had decided not to stage the promotion.

He said: "The Town Clerk told me in a nice way that I would not be welcome here and that was good enough for me."

*The canteen blaze at Aveling Barford*

## Bus driver saves firemen's blushes

A £2,000 blaze could have been worse but for the efforts of a bus driver.

As Aveling Barford's timber canteen went up in flames, firemen arrived at their station to go to the blaze - but there was not a driver among them.

They went next door to the bus station where Lincolnshire Road Car driver and local entertainer 'Tich' Godber offered his services.

Within a minute they were on their way.

The fire started in the afternoon when lightning struck an electric cable. It was fanned by the breeze and after an hour only the chimney stack remained.

Two billiard tables and a grand piano were lost in the blaze.

Mrs Ridley and Mrs Chantry were drinking tea in the kitchen when the fire started, unaware of the risk they were under.

Mrs Chantry said: "The lights went out so we phoned straight away for an electrician.

"Then we looked into the main hall and found it ablaze."

The ladies lost their hats and coats in the fire.

## Airmen cheat death in farm crash

PILOT Flt Lt J J Watts and Acting Pilot Officer G T Palmer, a King's School boarder, defied death when their Hart two-seater aircraft ploughed into a wall at Spittlegate Heath.

Both sustained concussion and slight injuries.

The front of the aircraft was wrecked although the rear was hardly damaged.

Before coming to rest, the wing caught the edge of a barn, damaging its roof, and the undercarriage was broken off. The plane was preparing to land at RAF Flying Training School, Grantham, shortly before midnight. It was put down to misjudgement.

Farmer Mr Griffin and his wife slept through and were unaware of the accident until the following morning.

# 1937 Grantham in the News

## Swindler jailed for lodging con

SALES manager Percy Charles Cavander was jailed for 18 months for what judge Mr Justice Humphries said was swindling poor people.

At Lincoln Assizes the 59-year-old had denied allegations of fraud by obtaining food and lodgings worth £2.72 from café owner Alfred Barnett, of London Road, Grantham, and Eugene Odling, of the Bridge Hotel, Westgate, Grantham.

Cavender stayed several days at Barnett's café, leaving a worthless IOU.

He also borrowed 75p from Mr Odling, which he continually assured him would be repaid 'tomorrow'.

The accused said he had fallen on hard times and intended to repay the money. The court heard he had six previous convictions.

## Preacher shouted down during celebrations

AN outburst interrupted a sermon as the Grantham and District Free Church Council celebrated its 60th anniversary.

All denominations gathered for the Diamond Jubilee, at the Wesleyan Church, Bridge End Road, as the Rev Wilfrid L Hannan gave his sermon.

But when he suggested the congregation took out pen and paper to jot down the name of a book, a young man called out: "A lot of tommy rot."

He continued: "If there are any Christians in here I hope they will back me up."

As the preacher tried to continue, the young man went on to say: "I cannot sit here and listen to this nonsense."

With that he left.

## Mobile plant firm moves

THE Dysart Road factory which until its recent closure was occupied by Potter Pumps, was sold to Ealing company R H Neal for £3,000.

The new company manufactured mobile plant and cranes which would be made at Grantham.

The factory had 3,000sq m of floor space and six acres of land.

The factory was built in the 19th Century, by Hemstead's.

## Fire rated

OFFICIAL records were saved when fire broke out at the town council's rates office, thanks to fireman Walter Kirk.

Mr Kirk, a corporation employee who lived on the premises, discovered the outbreak and called the fire brigade, stationed at the nearby Guildhall.

Chemical fire extinguishers were used as water would have destroyed the records.

## Golf club secure

RUMOURS that Grantham Golf Club was about to close were scotched when it signed a new lease with its landowners.

Based at Harrowby Without, the club agreed a three-year tenancy deal with owners the Land Settlements Association in place of the annual one.

---

**GENTLEMEN !**
Are you thinking of Buying a **NEW SUIT** for this Spring ?

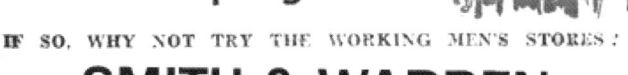

IF SO, WHY NOT TRY THE WORKING MEN'S STORES:

**SMITH & WARREN**
**13 & 14 CASTLEGATE, GRANTHAM**

WE HAVE READY-MADES from 17.6 and MANY PATTERNS from which to choose for MADE-TO-MEASURES.
SEND US A CARD and our Representative will be pleased to come and MEASURE YOU IN YOUR OWN HOME, TOWN OR COUNTRY.
LADIES.—We are now in a position to offer MADE-TO-MEASURE COATS and COSTUMES !
Join the Ranks of the Increasing Number of our Satisfied Customers !
OUR ONLY ADDRESS:
**13 & 14 CASTLEGATE**

# Grantham in the News — 1937

## Controversial book is withdrawn

A BOOK written by a Harlaxton man in which many of the characters were said to be based on Grantham's leading citizens, was banned.

Rotten Borough, by Julian Pine – real name Oliver Anderson - was doing good business in Grantham bookshops, until the intervention of Lord Brownlow.

Publisher Bernard Watson "expressed his regret that any misunderstanding may have arisen."

He also spoke to Mayor of Grantham Arthur Eatch, MP Sir Victor Warrener, and other civic dignitaries.

Mr Anderson, the son of a former Little Ponton vicar, said: "In the view of the wildly farcical nature of the work and its impossible extravagancies, it never occurred to me that anyone in the Grantham area or anywhere else, could possibly consider themselves being depicted."

## Crowded coach

A LINCOLNSHIRE Road Car bus driver was fined £5 and his conductor £1 for aiding and abetting after admitting overloading their vehicle.

When stopped on the Grantham to Oakham route, he was carrying 44 passengers, 20 more than allowed.

## Blind dog was no retriever

A BLIND dog was called as a witness before Spittlegate Court when Claypole farmer Arthur Revill was cleared of failing to have a dog licence.

It was claimed Mr Revill's dog - exempt from holding a licence - retrieved a pheasant.

Mr Revill, who was discharged, told magistrates: "This dog is absolutely blind and useless for sporting purposes."

*The parade marches along a wet and dismal High Street*

## Rain whets the town's appetite for Coronation fun

LAVISHLY decorated vehicles of all descriptions paraded through Grantham's streets to celebrate the coronation of King George VI.

It was led by young men wearing gigantic carnival heads.

But their efforts were spoiled by a day-long downpour. Crowds who braved the weather to watch were drenched to the skin.

A tap and ballet dance display to be held in the bandstand on St Peter's Hill, was moved into the Guildhall.

The Duke of Rutland took over the Picture House cinema the following day for tenants and employees to watch Grantham's first screening in town of the Coronation.

Letters poured in from all over the country declaring Grantham as the prettiest and best decorated town on the Great North Road.

Decorations were festooned everywhere, the town council alone putting up six miles of garlands.

Pick of the residential decorated streets were among the less well off. Paradise Place, Newbatt's Place, Malt Hill, Railway Terrace, Harrow Street and Rutland Street were all outstanding.

A massive bonfire on Beacon Hill was lit by top Hollywood film star and former Danish lightweight boxing champion Carl Brisson.

Outside the town, the Coronation was celebrated with equal vigour, except at Denton where adult sports was cancelled due to the rain and a measles and chicken pox epidemic which kept children at home.

# 1937 Grantham in the News

## More patients

A REPORT revealed that 1,080 inpatients were treated at Grantham Hospital in the past year, 25 of them victims of road accidents.

## Airman jailed

A 19-year-old aircraftman of RAF Cranwell was jailed for one month for stealing a car owned by Dr James Hopper, of Avenue Road, Grantham.

## Farming goods end

THE manufacture of agricultural implements by Ruston and Hornsby ended at Grantham.

After announcing a profit of £140,906 at its Grantham, Lincoln and Stockport works, the company said it would concentrate on making engines, boilers and pumps at Grantham.

## Tyred out

TYRESOLE, a company which remoulded tyres, was launched by Mr Lou Morley at North Road Garages, Great Ponton.

## King's College

THE Town Council was looking to form a technical college in town, using existing buildings at the King's School.

## New bell in place

A NEW 350kg bell was hoisted into place at Grantham Guildhall, thanks to a donation by Miss A G Green of Welby Gardens.

The bell had a deeper tone than the 1831 bell which it replaced.

**Workmen constructing the balcony of the new cinema in March**

## Cinema opens for business

THE State Cinema (later the Granada) opened for business in October, with The Plainsman, starring Gary Cooper, the first film to be shown.

It was opened by the Mayor of Grantham, Coun Arthur Eatch.

The biggest cinema in town, it had 1,500 seats including an extensive balcony.

There were also more than 1,000 light bulbs.

The Compton organ was inaugurated by top organist Reginald New. Manager B J Land said there had been 145 applications for jobs there.

## Expensive fuel

A LUMP of coal worth less than 4p cost a Grantham man £2 when he appeared before Bourne magistrates, even though the case against him was dismissed.

Charles Bailey, of North Parade, was driving through Folkingham in his Austin Seven, when he saw the lump of coal, weighing about 20kg, lying in the road. He stopped and put it in his boot.

But the coal had fallen from the back of a steamroller and witnesses who saw Mr Bailey took his registration number and reported his actions.

Mr Bailey said he realised he had been foolish. He had already burned the coal.

Magistrates dismissed the case on payment of £2 costs.

## Turned on by wireless

PEOPLE in the Grantham area became big fans of the radio.

A total of 6,885 licences were issued compared with 6,526 the previous year. Of these, 3,648 were sold through Grantham's General Post Office.

This meant more than half of the town's 6,000 homes were switched on.

One reason for an increase in licence was the previous year's purge on pirate listeners.

# Grantham in the News      1937

*Unity House under construction earlier in the year*

## New Co-op shop opens

UNITY House, the Grantham Equitable Co-operative Society's new emporium on the corner of London Road and St Catherine's Road, was opened by chairman of the English Co-operative Wholesale Society, Sir William Bradshaw, of Grantham.

But due to poor weather, the December opening had to be made inside the building.

The new store, incorporating chemists Boots, brought a number of departments under one roof.

But the extension was not without difficulties.

A sewer was discovered running under the existing building which had to be shored up.

Faults were also discovered in the roof and it had to be replaced.

Formed in 1872, the society had 6,734 members. It was originally in Inner Street, then Wharf Road, and High Street, until it settled on St Peter's Hill.

This was the society's biggest expansion since 1908 when it opened the Springfield Road shop, a bakery on Bridge End Road and a slaughterhouse.

## Life with the lions

TOP circus lion tamer 'Daredevil Dick' spent two weeks' holiday at his parents home in Manthorpe Road, Grantham.

Dick Foster, a cousin of Deputy Mayor of Grantham, Stanley Foster, was a top attraction in the circus ring before retiring to take on the role of superintendent of Belfast Zoo.

## Worst storms in modern memory

TWO cloudbursts in less than two months brought havoc to the town. In May, 1.5cm of rain fell in nine minutes.

Sidney Street and the Brook Street area were worst hit with many manhole covers forced off and cellars flooded.

Mr and Mrs G Bates, of 3 Sidney Street, were especially hard hit. Rain poured through their roof, bringing down ceilings and wrecking furniture and carpets.

In July, 5cm fell in an hour, bringing down trees, roofs and causing £1,000s damage.

## Sexton jailed for shooting neighbour

GRAVEDIGGER James Ablitt (39) of Uplands Drive, Grantham, was sentenced to three years penal servitude after admitting wounding his next-door neighbour.

He pleaded guilty to intent to grievous bodily harm at Lincoln Assizes, only six weeks later.

He admitted shooting Horace Wright as he got off his bike but denied he intended to kill him.

---

**MIDLAND BUILDERS MERCHANT Co., Ltd.,**
WHARF ROAD
GRANTHAM

We have in stock at Grantham and Newark over a hundred TILED SURROUNDS and COMBINATION GRATES, which you are cordially invited to inspect at any time without obligation to purchase.

**NOW IS THE TIME TO BUY THAT NEW GRATE you want before Spring Cleaning.**

**BUY BRITISH GOODS LOCALLY**

# 1938 Grantham in the News

*Bland's new buses in Westgate*

### Snow joke

FORMER Mayor of Grantham, Coun Richard Brittain broke an arm when he slipped and fell heavily on his garden path which was covered in snow.

## Bland sight for bus lovers

THE fleet of Bland's Pullman coaches which were the latest luxury on the road, were lined up in Wide Westgate for a promotional photograph.

Each bus had large pneumatic tyres and brakes on all four rear wheels.

## Rector in ducking threat

THE Rector of Pickworth, the Rev Thomas Ivens, was threatened with being thrown into the village duck pond by two of his parishioners.

The row was over the village social hall, which was built in the rectory grounds by permission of the previous incumbent the Rev St John Wright.

Things came to a head when farmer Ernest Topps and his son-in-law Charles Beecham claimed this meant the rectory drive was a right of way to the hall.

When the Rector denied this was the case, he was threatened with a ducking.

Bourne magistrates threw out the case and villagers agreed to move the hall elsewhere.

---

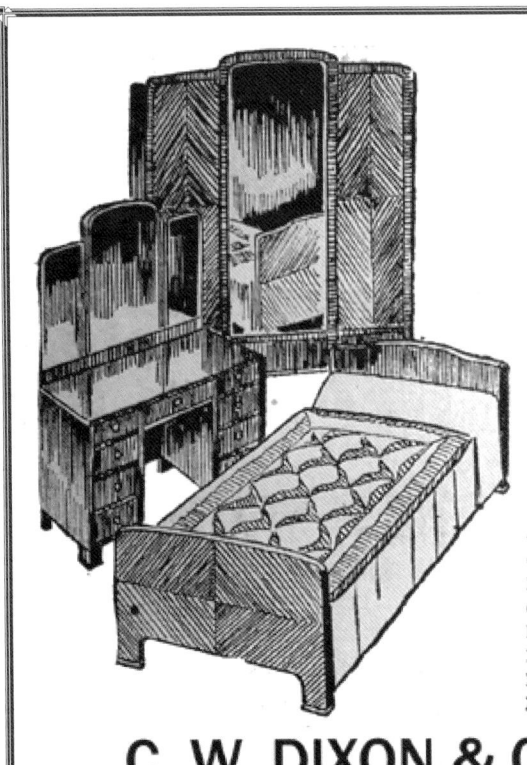

**OAK BEDROOM SUITES**

AT

various prices to suit all purchasers

▼

SEE OUR WINDOWS
FOR
GLASS
CHINA
DOWN QUILTS
CUSHIONS
PYREX WARE
FIRESIDE CHAIRS
DINNER WAGGONS
MIRRORS

**C. W. DIXON & Co.**
(FURNISHERS) Ltd
67, Wharf Road, Grantham

# Grantham in the News — 1938

## Horrific find by Ropsley schoolboy

AN 11-year-old boy made a grisly find when he returned to his Ropsley home.

In the bedroom, he discovered the mutilated body of his mother with his dying stepfather.

The woman, Eleanor Hannah Turfitt (32) had been cut and battered about the head.

A bloodstained woodsman's axe lay nearby. By her side, her husband Thomas Suter Turfitt (57) lay in a pool of blood with his throat cut, a carving knife in his hand. He was still alive.

The boy dashed from the house holding the axe and found May Harrison, who was feeding chickens.

He told her what he had found and the village doctor and policeman were called.

Mr Turfitt, a woodsman employed at Humby Hall was taken to the County Institution, Hill View, Grantham, where he died shortly afterwards.

The inquest of the Ropsley man was told Mr Turfitt had a very jealous nature.

He was liable to turn angry if anyone smiled at his wife or if he found her talking or laughing with someone.

The jury recorded that Mrs Turfitt died of her wounds and Mr Turfitt took his own life while the balance of his mind was disturbed.

## Holy smoke! We're on fire

A CHURCH roof burst into flames while worshippers were at evensong.

Timbers at St Swithun's Church, Long Bennington, were well alight when the Rev F C Hamblyn spotted them as he began his sermon.

Churchwarden George Dawson ran to get a ladder while the congregation said prayers before leaving orderly.

They then joined choristers to form a bucket chain outside and brought the fire under control before firemen arrived.

A spark from the church's heating system was blamed, with damage estimated at £50.

## A hole lot of trouble

A WOMAN injured in a road fall failed in her action at the King's Bench Division of the High Court against Grantham Corporation.

Louise Rudd, of Walton-on-Thames, Surrey, was walking with her 84-year-old mother, Mrs Patman along Dysart Road, when they both fell into a hole made by road repairers.

She injured her pelvis and joints which led to rheumatism.

Her husband also claimed £117 for medical attention to his wife

Mrs Rudd said they stepped to one side as a car approached them and fell into the hole.

Roadman Walter Kirk said there were 38 red lamps around the hole.

*The factory being built on Springfield Road*

## Another major factory opens

A FACTORY for a new company, British Manufacturing and Research Co (BMARCo) being built on Springfield Road, Grantham, was expected to bring 150 jobs to town.

Denis Kendall, an engineer of high reputation, was appointed general manager.

Previously works manager of Citroen, Paris, he had run away to sea at 14, earned $5,000 as a police informer on China's opium dens and ran a waterfront cabaret in Shanghai.

Mr Kendall then surfaced as a steeplejack in the USA before moving to a car plant there and then on to Paris.

# 1938 Grantham in the News

## Farm wages stable

FARM workers continued to be paid £1.73 per week following an agreement with the Kesteven and Lindsey Agricultural Wages Board.

Shepherds received £1.97 per week and wagoners £2.08. The rates applied to farm workers over 21.

But workers' call for a cut from a 54-hour week in summer and 56 hours in winter were rejected.

## Tuns of damage

PROMPT action by Three Tuns landlord George Walton, of Kirkby Underwood, prevented his thatched pub from going up in flames.

The fire caused extensive damaged to the bar and a pet budgerigar died. Mr Walton fought the fire with buckets of water drawn from the well until firemen arrived. The cause was unknown.

## Unready for raids

GRANTHAM was behind the rest of the UK for air raid precautions, the borough council was told.

Coun Stanley Foster said he had applied to the Government for the borough council to conduct its own affairs but was told it must go in with the county council scheme.

## Milk bar kids

GRANTHAM opened its first real milk bar in Butchers' Row.

Owned by Arthur Ellis, who also owned an ice cream factory on Dysart Road, it supported the national keep fit campaign.

*Carnival Queen Nellie Stockdale with her entourage*

## Carnival cuts hospital debt

NELLIE Stockdale was elected Grantham Hospital's Carnival Queen.

She headed a parade of floats through town.

Nellie (25) beat more than 100 rivals to take the title. Runner-up was Bertha Lord, of Ancaster.

Maids of honour were Joan Widdowson, of Great Ponton, Eileen Pullen, of Grantham, Evelyn Olive, of Walcot and Grace Dewey, of Croxton Kerrial.

They all wore dresses designed and made by haberdashers Arthur Chambers, of High Street, Grantham.

The carnival began in Westgate, then along Wharf Road, St Peter's Hill and High Street before finishing in the Market Place.

It raised nearly £2,000 towards paying off the hospital's £22,000 debt.

## Neighbours in fall out

A RESIDENT of Corporation Cottages, Belton Lane, Grantham, was fined £1 for assaulting his neighbour.

The defendant came to the woman's back door. When she asked him what he wanted, he said "I want you" and punched her on the jaw knocking her on to the kitchen table.

The defendant said the woman had spat in his wife's face and struck her, which the woman denied.

His version of the visit to his neighbours was that she struck him on the head repeatedly with a saucepan.

## New boss for cinema

THE State Cinema, St Peter's Hill, appointed Welshman Harry Sanders as manager. He succeeded A Fraser Green.

As manager of the Lido, Islington, Mr Sanders discovered world-famous child actor Freddie Bartholomew.

# Grantham in the News — 1938

## Over-forties barred from council jobs

LOCAL Government advertising vacancies for men not over 40 were condemned by old soldiers of Grantham British Legion.

They said it debarred anyone who had served in the war.

Men who had signed up for 21 years in the armed forces couldn't work for the council.

One delegate said: "During the war, the Army age limit was 51.

"We were not too old to fight but now the council says that's far too old to push a pen.

"We should press for a law that no councillor should be aged over 40."

Branch president Sir Ernest Sleight said he would fight until the maximum age for employment was at least 50.

**Ken Beck (front) and Sid Bradley**

## Boys build hot wheels

KEN Beck and Sid Bradley built their own fun car.

The picture was taken in Blue Lion Yard, off Market Place, where Sid's elder brother was licensee.

Both were in their teens and apprentices at Aveling Barford.

Ken's brother Maurice said: "Sparks came off the rear wheels when it was driven through Union Street.

Maurice said: "He still owes me 2.5p for the gallon of petrol he sent me to buy."

## New world steam record for LNER at Little Bytham

THE world record speed for a steam locomotive was shattered by LNER just south of Grantham.

Mallard, no 4468, designed by Sir Nigel Gresley, made the recording breaking run at Little Bytham, just 11 minutes after leaving Grantham station.

Driven by Joe Duddington with fireman Tom Bray, the A4 Pacific left King's Cross, London, on a scheduled run.

Everything was shrouded in secrecy. At Barkston, the train turned round for its record breaking run.

Mr Duddington said afterwards: "We didn't think we would do it. We crawled through Grantham at 24mph because of line repairs. By Great Ponton we were back on target."

Just south of Little Bytham the train reached 126mph, taking the world record from a German locomotive, which had reached an averaged 124.5mph in 1936.

A Little Bytham villager said: "Coal was leaping off the tender and was like shrapnel as the train went through the station. It was very exciting."

The previous LNER record was set in 1934 on the same stretch by the Flying Scotsman.

## House struck by lightning

MORE than 70 tonnes of rain to the acre fell in Billingborough during a raging storm.

At nearby Folkingham, the main street was flooded and two houses struck by lightning.

A chimney pot was shattered and the room below filled with soot and sulphurous fumes.

A row of council houses in Pickworth Road was also struck, damaging the roof and stripping the tiles of Mr and Mrs Dodds' home.

The house was flooded by rain.

A bull and cow sheltering under a hedge were killed and an ash tree set alight by lightning.

73

# 1938 Grantham in the News

## Youth saved men from smoke-filled home

A SIXTEEN-year-old youth was rewarded after saving the lives of two men on his way to work.

Mayor of Grantham Stanley Foster presented him with a framed certificate and a £2 cheque awarded by the Protection of Life from Fire.

Reginald Kightley was on his way to work as a dairyman with the Co-op at 6.15am when he saw smoke issuing from a ground floor window.

He heard coughing, and when there was no response to his knocking, he forced open the front door. In a smoke-filled room, he found Robert Charity, 76, on his back.

A second man, asleep upstairs, was alerted by Reginald's knocking and fled to safety.

Mr Foster said: "The town is very proud of you."

## Short of beds for new mums

GRANTHAM Hospital was desperate for a new maternity block, the governors' annual meeting was told.

Chairman Rothwell Lee said it was urgent as there were only 10 beds in the labour ward serving a population of 40,000.

Alderman Lee also told the meeting it cost £3.29 a week to keep a patient in the hospital.

The average stay was three weeks.

## Higher profits

RUSTON and Hornsby chairman Col J S Ruston said he was pessimistic for the company's future, despite record-breaking profits.

Announcing profits of £243,000 he told the annual meeting: "Unless we are favoured with a period of political peace abroad it is hard to see how we can hope to maintain our order books at this level."

## Man dies after fall

FARMWORKER Arthur Beecham, 65, died of head injuries after falling from the drum of a threshing machine at Welby. He overbalanced after being struck by a sudden gust of wind.

## Air raid appeal

POSTERS appealing for volunteers to become air-raid wardens were put up around the town.

## New castle

VIOLET Van der Elst of Harlaxton Manor, renamed her home Grantham Castle.

## Marriage bliss

MURIEL Redman, 18, of Billingborough, was given permission by Bourne magistrates to marry her intended after her mother refused to give consent.

They said Cpl George Walter, an Air Force policeman, could afford to keep her.

---

We are in the News at "No 1"

**WATERGATE WIDENING**

BUT....

So long as we are in business (and we think it will be quite a time yet) we shall continue to give our best as to Style and Value.

You can rely on the QUALITY AT SHARPLEY'S.
COATS :: COSTUMES :: BLOUSES :: MILLINERY
GLOVES and HOSIERY

**D & H. Sharpley**
"No 1" HIGH STREET
GRANTHAM

# Grantham in the News — 1938

## Top cop spells out the danger of gas masks

IGNORANCE of gasmasks worried Grantham's top cop, Chief Constable Weatherhogg.

He said: "We've even had a case of a 14-year-old boy who put his on then climbed into a live gas oven to test it.

"That was an extremely dangerous practice. It could have had serious consequences."

The threat of war having accelerated, air raid precautions led everyone over the age of four to be issued with a gasmask.

The public were warned to keep their gasmasks dry and away from heat and light. They were instructed to rub a film of soap over the inside of the glass to stop it misting up.

Straps had to be properly adjusted to ensure that all air was breathed through the filter.

Mr Weatherhogg said: "The best place to be in an air raid is a gas-proof room. One should be prepared in every household."

## Jail for beggar who showed his scars

THOMAS George James was jailed for 14 days after being found guilty of obtaining alms by exposing wounds or deformities.

Pc Elmer told Grantham magistrates he saw James in the Market Place.

He said he was holding a box in his right hand with a notice which said 'Crippled in the arm; my only means at present'.

His left arm was exposed from the elbow showing a scar. He had a deformed arm, wrist and hand.

When spoken to by the officer, he became abusive and threw the box to the ground. It contained 6p.

## Not white

A LABOURER from Harrowby Land Settlements, was fined 50p by Spittlegate magistrates for riding a bicycle without a white surface on the mudguard.

## Bride dies in blaze

A SPROXTON man's bride, who lived in Coventry, died while having her pre-wedding photograph taken.

The woman and two bridesmaids burned to death when the dress of one of the girls caught in an electric fire. The bride and three other attendants rushed to beat the flames out only for their own dresses to catch fire.

The girl died shortly afterwards and the bride and a six-year-old bridesmaid died later.

## Fined for taking spuds

NINETEEN potato pickers from Grantham were each fined 25p for their part in stealing potatoes from farmer Henry Burtt, of Dunsby.

Bourne magistrates were told the foreman had told the pickers that no potatoes could be taken home.

They took about 55kg of them worth £1.60.

Magistrate T W Pinder said he could understand the odd potato being stolen but some people had taken nearly 12kg.

They were stopped by police and they returned home along Billingborough Road.

One of the defendants said the potatoes were very small and would have been left in the field to rot had they not taken them.

**MEMBERS of the Gingerbread Carnival formed this year. From left are Miss G. Baxter Mr H Welbourne, Mr B Abbot and Mr P Aspland**

# 1939 Grantham in the News

## New school opens

ST Wulfram's Infant School was formally opened on New Beacon Road in July although children had moved in a month earlier, from Brownlow School, Castlegate.

## Barford's flat out

ANNOUNCING profits of £71,722, chairman Edward Barford told Aveling Barford shareholders the Grantham plant was working at full capacity.

He said this was despite difficulties in the export markets.

## Taste for crime

BURGLARS who broke into the Picture House cinema, St Peter's Hill, left empty handed after searching the premises.

But they didn't leave hungry. They made themselves ham sandwiches and helped themselves to cakes in the cafe.

## Catching the tube

THE town council agreed to replace the open trenches used for sheltering from air raids with 20 two-metre diameter tubes buried underground.

They each protected 100 people from gas attacks and bombs.

## Year end Jobless up

GRANTHAM'S unemployment figures for December showed a massive increase over the previous month - 716 against 544.

The full figures, with November's in brackets, were: Men 505 (413) boys 15 (5), women 156 (91) and girls 40 (35).

## Conflict with Hitler not inevitable - town MP

GRANTHAM MP Sir Victor Warrender said he still refused to believe war was inevitable so long as there was a Prime Minister of the calibre and character of Mr Chamberlain.

Mr Warrender, financial secretary to the War Office, was speaking in Lincoln.

He had flown from London to Waddington in his private plane before completing his journey to Grantham by car.

He said: "The Tories have got to anticipate a General Election in the not too distant future.

"If there was a man in the country today who deserves admiration and sympathy it is Neville Chamberlain."

He criticised those who advocated a "preventative war" declaring that if war broke out tomorrow, they would probably be the first to cry "halt" when the trouble started.

## Landlord and his wife obstruct police during raid

THE landlord and landlady of the Blue Man pub, Grantham, battled with police to stop them taking away glasses from after-hours boozers.

The three officers entered the Westgate pub at 11.20pm, 80 minutes after it should have closed. Twelve customers in various states of drunkenness were drinking.

Landlord George Whitehouse was fined £10 for serving after hours and £2 for obstructing police while four drinkers were fined £1 each.

The police saw a light on at the rear of the premises and entered. But when they tried to remove glasses, Mr Whitehouse and his wife tried to grab them.

They were warned they were aggravating the situation, but continued to struggle. One of the customers tried to restrain them.

As police left, Mrs Whitehouse shouted after them, saying she hoped they got a medal the size of a frying pan for their evening's work.

One of the officers, Pc Topps, said he believed Mrs Whitehouse was the worse for drink.

---

**A.R.P.**

BEDDING REQUIREMENTS

| | |
|---|---|
| 4ft. 6in. Spring Interior Mattress | 59/6 |
| 4ft. 6in. Sprung Base . . . . | 37/6 |
| 4ft. 6in. Wool Overlays . . . | 32/6 |
| 3ft. Wool Overlays . . . . | 22/6 |

SPECIAL ! ! !

| | |
|---|---|
| 3FT. Black Iron Comb. Beds . . | 24/6 |
| Black Bolton Sheeting. 74in. wide | 3/11 per yard |

**JOHN HALL**
LIMITED

**GRANTHAM**

# Grantham in the News — 1939

## Four killed in bomber crash

FOUR airmen attached to RAF Waddington lost their lives in a plane crash at Irnham.

Their bomber had been flying low over the fields when it crashed on the edge of a wood.

There was a terrific explosion which was heard as far away as Corby where windows were shaken.

The four airmen were blown to pieces over a 150m radius and all that remained of the aircraft was a mass of charred wreckage.

The casualties were: Flg Off David Jobson (26) of New Zealand, Sgt Plt John Archibald (26) of London, Act Sgt Ernest Jones (21) of London and radio operator Ac Ronald Andrews (21) from Kent.

Local gamekeeper Walter Partridge said he saw two aircraft flying very low, one of them no more than 50m above the ground.

He said: "This one dived straight into the ground."

## Dear greens

HERBERT Hall, of Dudley Road, was fined £1 and ordered to pay 50p costs by magistrates for stealing two cabbages from a neighbour's allotment off Manthorpe Road.

The stolen goods were worth less than 2p.

## New vicar for St Wulfram's

THE Rev Charles Harold Leeke, vicar of St Nicholas Church, Lincoln, was appointed Vicar of Grantham.

Lincoln-born, he was the son of Canon E T Leeke, chancellor and sub-dean of Lincoln Cathedral for many years. Mr Leeke (51) was married with three daughters.

Ordained in Lincoln Cathedral in 1911, he was curate at Boston until 1914. He spent 15 years with the Universities Mission to Central Africa.

*Grantham railway station prepared for air raids*

## Air raid warning sounds on day after war declared

WITHIN 24 hours of war being declared between Great Britain and Germany, Grantham had its first shock when air raid warnings sounded at 2.40am on Monday morning.

In the space of eight minutes of the warbling notes, all the ARP services had been called into operation from the report centre.

The response was exceptional.

Many ARP workers who had gone off duty less than an hour previously, returned to their posts with remarkable promptness.

Within 15 minutes of the call, the town's services were ready for any emergency which might have arisen.

Fortunately, they were not brought into action as the call, affecting most of the midlands, was a precautionary measure in view of unidentified aeroplanes heading for the east coast.

These proved to be friendly.

Although the ARP services did a sterling job, concern at behaviour of civilians was raised.

A number of them congregated on street corners and were even seen lighting cigarettes.

## Goods trains collide

TWO goods trains collided at Corby station blocking the main LNER line between Grantham and King's Cross for more than 12 hours.

There were no serious injuries although guard Robert Haylett, of Peterborough, had a miraculous escape when the van he was in was smashed to pieces.

The crash caused long delays to main line traffic which had to be diverted along the station's slow line.

# 1939 Grantham in the News

## Peace... or else

MRS Violet Van der Elst called for 20,000 women from all parts of the world to demand an end to warfare.

She took out advertisements in the national press claiming the power of women could end war for all time.

She invited them to join the Women's Peace Legion based at her Harlaxton home, Grantham Castle.

Mrs Van der Elst also bought two aeroplanes to display banners carrying the organisation's message.

She said: "If enough women say there will be no more war then there will be no more war.

"The men know what to expect if we turn down their demands and will soon give in to us."

*The march reaches the Guildhall*

## Old soldiers on the march for new recruits

A HIGH-power recruiting drive to get young people to sign up for the three armed services was held in May.

It began with a march featuring territorials, old comrades and new recruits, followed by gun carriers and tanks.

The parade was inspected by Lord Brownlow, the Mayor Ald Stanley Foster and Col Grinling.

Photographer Walter Lee said attitudes had suddenly changed.

He said: "It doesn't seem so long ago since the territorials wore civilian mackintoshes over their military uniforms rather than flaunt them."

## Bravery reward for vicar

A BRAVE deed by a Grantham clergyman was recognised by the Carnegie Hero Trust which gave a £15 reward to the Vicar of St Anne's Church.

The Rev Edwin Millard was in Scotland with his wife, three children and Mrs Wood (70), a parishioner who lived on Cold Harbour Lane.

Mrs Wood went to the edge of the cliff at the Falls of Falooch, Crianlarich, Perthshire, and tripped, falling into the deep swirling pool surrounded by deep precipitous rock.

Without a thought for his own safety, Mr Millard dived into the water and rescued her.

---

**THE GOVERNMENT APPEALS TO THE BRITISH FARMER TO**

*Plough up more acres*

You may be wondering how to tackle this extra work economically and may still be hesitant at the idea of employing Tractor power. Tractor power is the only practical method of ploughing up large acreage and of speeding up arable operations generally.

It will lower your production costs, providing that the Tractor itself is efficient and economical. On the strength of these two points, the Fordson, built by British workmen from British materials has won its position as "Britain's most popular Tractor"

**Fordson**
AGRICULTURAL TRACTOR

PRICES from £150 at Works
WE CAN give Good Delivery

**GRANTHAM TRACTOR Co., Ltd.**
The Main Fordson Dealers
26 LONDON ROAD, GRANTHAM

# Grantham in the News  1939

## Fire, falls and fainting at the fair

THERE was more fun at the Mid-Lent Fair than usual when an airman was tossed from one of the steam yachts.

Aircraftman Cooper suffered concussion and was taken back to his RAF station by ambulance after being treated by Red Cross volunteers.

Another man was taken to hospital with a foot injury from an unrelated incident.

The Red Cross said they had a busy fair with many instances of fainting.

On the final day, a fortune-teller's tent, in narrow Westgate, went up in flames.

Owner May Smith, of Granby Yard, Grantham, escaped unharmed.

A stove heater was blamed for the fire which was extinguished by police and public before it could spread to nearby attractions.

Wednesday was Hospital Night, when showmen handed over a percentage of their takings to Grantham Hospital.

**The Aveling Barford stand at Windsor**

## Jolly good show, Barford

FLEDGLING Grantham engineering company Aveling Barford was a big success at the Centenary Royal Show, in Windsor Great Park.

Some of the employees were on the company's stand as King George VI and Queen Elizabeth drove along the main avenue.

## Air Defence squadron formed.

FORTY-five lads aged 14 to 18 signed up for the new Air Defence Corps, one of the first squadrons formed in the country.

At a meeting at the Guildhall, £89 was collected for the scheme, expected to cost £350 in its first year.

The meeting was addressed by Marshal of the RAF Sir John M Salmond.

The Air League (later known as the Air Training Corps), which began the movement, hoped to attract 20,000 youths nationally and have 200 squadrons by the end of the year.

The Grantham squadron was to meet in a hut behind the post office.

## Initial reaction to shock birth

A BOY born at Grantham Hospital survived thanks to a quick thinking railway guard.

Jack Roberts, a Woolwich Arsenal engineer from Erith, Kent, was travelling to West Hartlepool with his pregnant wife when she went in to labour near Peterborough.

He notified the guard who threw out a message at Corby station, asking to stop the train at Grantham.

By chance, Dr James Hopper was giving a talk to the station staff ambulance staff and dealt with the emergency as soon as signalling staff stopped the train.

A 7lb baby was born soon afterwards at Grantham Hospital.

Mr Roberts said: "We were going to call him Jack, but we may now make his initials LNER as a reminder of this day."

## Police get phones

POLICE in the Grantham area were told they would get a telephone in every station.

The standing joint committee said it would be useful in an emergency.

Chairman Sir Robert Pattinson said: "If we are to be serious in our preparations for the emergency then it will have to be done."

He said the chief constable must be able to communicate with all stations.

# 1939 Grantham in the News

## Too young to retire at eighty-five

EDWIN Pidd (85) refused to retire after more than 70 years service with Ruston and Hornsby.

He said: "I mean to keep on working as long as I can. I hope they'll let me carry on a few more years yet."

Mr Pidd got up at 6.30am every day to go about his duties as yard foreman with vigour and enthusiasm.

He began working for 'the Firm' on Fair Monday 1867. Father of former Mayoress Mrs Eatch, he lived in Inner Street, next door to his work.

In his early days with the firm, he travelled all over the world including Russia, Germany, South Africa, Chile and Belgium.

He said: "I would do it all again given the chance."

Mr Pidd said his health was as good as it ever as. According to his wife, when he got up in the morning he was "singing like a lark."

Usually Mr Pidd went to bed at 8pm but was sometimes known to stay up as late as 10pm.

*Denton Manor's final days*

## Denton Manor demolished

DENTON Manor, which survived a major fire in 1906, was pulled down by its owners, the Welby family. The stately home had become too expensive to maintain.

## Girls' new head appointed

MISS Dorothy J C Gillies MA, was appointed headmistress of Kesteven and Grantham Girls' School.

Previously in charge of the classical department at Wolverhampton High School.

She succeeded Miss H G Williams, headteacher since the school opened in 1911.

## Carry on drinking

A CALL by churches for an end to the 30-minute summertime extension in drinking hours to 10.30pm was rejected by the licensing justices.

Mr J W Simmonds, of the Free Church Council, said it should be stopped in view of the grave international situation.

But Mayor Stanley Foster allowed it to continue, saying there was a reduction in drunkenness during the summer months.

## Air blue over red claim

AN amazing row between Mrs Violet Van der Elst, of Harlaxton, and Sir Stafford Cripps created a sensation at a meeting in support of Sir Stafford's campaign for a popular front movement.

It happened at the end of Sir Stafford's speech in Grantham's Westgate Hall. Mrs Van der Elst leaped from her seat and demanded to know why he had got her rejected as the prospective Labour candidate for Widnes.

Declaring her socialist principles, she accused Sir Stafford of being a Communist.

There was uproar for several minutes and despite cries of "sit down" she remained on her feet until Sir Stafford told her he would not answer her question until she was seated.

## Name dropping

ROPSLEY butcher Wilburt Slowen was fined £2 by borough magistrates for failing to display his name and address on his meat stall at Grantham market.

# Grantham in the News — 1940

## Fairground rides go up in flames

A BLAZE ripped through a fairground causing damage put at thousands of pounds.

John Farrar's fair, from Rotherham, was in the field behind the Journal's High Street printing works.

It was one of the biggest fires in the town for years.

The Noah's Ark, dodgems, coconut shies and side shows, made mainly of wood and canvas, were engulfed in flames.

Members of the AFS (Auxiliary Fire Service) arrived within two minutes of being called but strong winds put the blaze out of control.

Instead, firemen concentrated on keeping the flames away from nearby houses and the Journal where several tonnes of newsprint were stored.

The fire was caused by an overheating engine.

## Hard labour for refusing light task

A 68-year-old man staying at Grantham Institution, Dysart Road, was jailed for a month with hard labour for refusing to carry out his allotted task.

On his first day he was ordered to sweep out the casual ward, which he did.

But on the second day, he refused to sweep the mortuary.

John Raby, of Manchester, said: "It's so ridiculous, it's just a farce."

*The east side of Ruston & Hornsby after the bombing raid*

## Seven killed as Germans step up bombing raids

SEVEN people were killed and 16 injured when four high-explosive bombs hit London Road.

It was the fifth raid on Grantham, although previous bombs had fallen harmlessly in outlying fields.

On September 30, a south-flying German bomber hit Ruston and Hornsby's east side works, destroying the erection shop and drawing office.

Nearby Parker's shop, the Joiners Arms and Steel and Hubbard's garage were razed to the ground.

Fourteen other buildings were damaged with a further 351 suffering slight damage including Fred Bates' shop window, on Wharf Road, which was shattered.

Hornsby's erection shop was hit by the first bomb and the drawing office by the second.

The third fell into the road outside Parker's shop and the Joiners.

The final bomb hit the garage in the Manners' Arms yard. It brought tiles from the pub and the Spotted Cow opposite crashing down.

ARP volunteers were caught by surprise. They were meeting at the Guildhall and at first ignored the raid.

Suddenly the building was rocked and the wardens saw a red glow over Hornsby's.

London Road became congested with sightseers, hindering the efforts of rescuers and firefighters.

## Ex-Mayor slams cost of housing

A FORMER mayor protested at the proposed cost of new council houses.

Coun Arthur Eatch, himself a builder, said he believed at £700 each they were far too expensive for the town to bear.

A report by the borough surveyor said the housing committee accepted the lowest tender, which was by Rudd and Son of Grantham.

The 250 houses were to be built on the Cherry Orchard estate.

# 1940 Grantham in the News

## Soldier's death announcement was premature

A SOLDIER whose death had been announced in the Grantham Journal was found to be alive in Germany.

Pte Rupert Gibson, of Great Gonerby, who married in April, was reported missing believed killed in Norway later that month.

His widow Cassie had mourned his loss and placed an obituary in the local paper.

But in July, it was announced he was wounded and a prisoner of war in Germany.

Mr Gibson, who worked for the Co-op and played football with Thursday Wolves, was a territorial with the Lincolnshire Regiment.

## Water supply hit by bomb

A GERMAN bomber scored a direct hit on both of Grantham's trunk water mains.

But thanks to the foresight of installing a water tower on Gorse Lane, the town was hardly affected. Grantham Waterworks chairman Dr Shipman said: "They were both blown out of the ground but in a matter of 30 minutes they were turned off.

"Grantham was one of the few, if not the only town to have its trunk main bombed yet maintained its supply."

He said the mains from the 100,000-gallon water tower originally stopped at Belvoir Avenue, although the Ministry of Health immediately sanctioned it to continue to Westgate following the bombing.

## Trinity turn down Town

GAINSBOROUGH Trinity players refused to turn out for a Midland League fixture at Grantham.

They said Grantham failed to fulfil their fixture at Gainsborough the previous season.

The players had the backing of the club's board.

Manager C H Caldicott said: "We've played a string of away fixtures in the past few weeks and have only taken £45 in gate money.

"We can hardly afford to travel to Grantham."

A Grantham spokesman said they would have been prepared to switch the fixture had they been given more notice.

## Gas leak kills baby and puts family in hospital

AN 11-month baby boy died and five other members of the family were taken to hospital with gas poisoning.

They were discovered when a customer went to their Springfield Road shop.

Finding the door locked, and getting no response to his knocking, he called the police.

Inspector Bond and Sgt Ledger found the owners, Mr and Mrs Osborne unconscious, together with Malcolm (6) Sylvia (6), Brian (8) and the dead baby.

The cause of the tragedy was a gas main which had been cracked by the frost.

Escaping gas permeated through the cellar, the shop and finally the bedrooms.

## Car was too mobile

FOR failing to immobilise his car in Stamford Street, under wartime regulations, an engine tester was fined £1.50 by the borough court.

---

### THE ALL STEEL RALEIGH

The "old-timers'" bogey that cycling entails hard work can be dismissed from the mind, as the lighter and more scientifically designed frame, the livelier tyres and easier running bearings, has made it a speedier and easier business than walking, and in the

### ALL STEEL RALEIGH

which has taken the lead in every cycling innovation for fifty years,

**ALL THESE DESIRABLE FEATURES ARE INCORPORATED**

Prices from
**£6-3-9**
or with 3-Speed gear from
**£7-7-6**

18/- Deposit and 11/7 per Month

### FRED BATES
CYCLES & RADIO
WHARF ROAD
GRANTHAM

# Grantham in the News 1940

## Seven-shot Eddie scares off garage raiders

A GUN-toting garage owner chased off raiders from his premises.

It happened after Eddie Collin, owner of Roman Garage, Bridge End Road, near Grantham, was woken from his sleep at about 1.20am.

Mr Collin said: "I grabbed a revolver I keep under my pillow and gave my wife a shotgun. She went to the cafe and I went to the showroom where £1,000 worth of tyres were stored."

Mrs Collin heard a noise outside and the couple went to look.

They saw a driver starting up a Morris car having stolen 25 litres of petrol.

Mr Collin said: "As they drove off, I fired at the front tyre but missed.

"In their escape the raiders drove over a metre high bank and grazed a telegraph pole.

"I gave them six rounds from the revolver but missed."

Police confirmed afterwards that the car was stolen.

## No conchies on council

COUNTY council chairman Sir Robert Pattinson said no council employees had registered as conscientious objectors.

"They are all patriotic and realise that our freedom is worth defending." he said.

"Otherwise they would be dealt with."

*New homes under construction*

## Homes being built

TWO-hundred-and-twenty-seven homes were being built in Beeden Park, nicknamed Garden City.

The homes were of the most modern design, with flat roofs.

Each house would have front and back gardens, with a large central playing area and trees in the street.

The first completed were for workers associated with the war effort.

The council accepted the lowest tender for the scheme which was from Hustwayte, of Nottingham, of £128,487.

## Drive for scrap

A BIG salvage drive was launched in town, just two weeks after Coun Arthur Eatch was appointed chairman of the salvage sub-committee.

The main materials required for recycling were waste paper and cardboard, scrap metal, rags, bones and bottles.

They were collected by two freighters with a special 'boom' week for each class of material.

Each freighter had a driver and 12 volunteer schoolboys.

## Where's the fire?

PROMPT action by neighbours saved a cottage next door to a fire station from destruction.

They saw smoke billowing from the roof of Mr King's home in Old Rectory Cottages, Folkingham, and raked it out by removing tiles.

Jackdaws were blamed for bringing in debris.

Neighbours tried to get into the old fire station but the doors were jammed. The equipment was also badly maintained and didn't work.

## Garden soiled by bullock

SCRAP dealer Charles Spick was awarded £1.25 by Grantham County Court after a bullock caused chaos in his garden.

He claimed £2 after the beast, owned by farmer William Harris, of Grantley Street, broke through a hedge and scraped up potatoes, beans, carrots, sprouts and leeks.

Mr Harris said: "I offered him a joint of beef but he refused it."

# 1940 Grantham in the News

## School closed for war

WELBY Street School was closed until the end of hostilities.

The 80-year-old school saw numbers dwindle to the extent that the number of children did not justify the expense.

## Books returned

THE books in St Wulfram's Church chained library, which had been removed to a place of supposed greater safety, were returned to the church.

## Wife's tragic death

A YOUNG wife died after an empty hot water tank exploded in her bathroom.

Evelyn Samuel (26) was investigating a strange noise at her Bottesford home.

The explosion blew out doors and windows.

## Duke dies

JOHN Henry Montague Manners, ninth Duke of Rutland, died of pneumonia at Belvoir Castle. He was 53.

He succeeded his father to the title in 1925.

He was an expert on medieval art.

## Purge on rats

A COUNTYWIDE campaign against rats destroyed 29,872 of them in the last three months of the year.

The attack was backed by the Lincolnshire branch of the National Farmers' Union.

## Woman claims damages after Co-op trap door fall

AN ILFORD woman was awarded £530 at Nottinghamshire Assizes in her action against Grantham Equitable Co-operative Industrial Society.

Roberta Whyte (54) visited the shop while on holiday with her sister at Bingham.

It was a dull afternoon and there were no lights.

Miss Whyte, who was short-sighted, walked straight over to the assistant working at the meat block and fell through an open trap door.

She broke both of her wrists.

The floor was dark and there was no light in the cellar.

Miss Whyte told the judge Mr Justice Oliver: "I had to be washed and fed for several weeks. My grip is still weak."

Co-op president Walter Barnes said: "The trap door has been in use since 1913 and there's been no record of an accident before."

He admitted that nothing had been done since to make the trap door safer.

Shop assistant Percy Money, of Edward Street, said: "In all the years I worked here, no customer went to the meat block before."

## Put up obstacles farmers told

FARMERS were urged to put obstacles on their land to prevent enemy aircraft using it to land.

Commissioner for the Region, Lord Trent, called for patriotism and self-preservation.

He said after a voluntary period, the military will inspect farms and carry out necessary work themselves.

He warned that if farmers did it themselves there was less chance of damage to crops than if the military moved in.

He said any field with 300m put to grass must have obstacles from posts to farm implements.

"Anything likely to damage an aircraft."

## Carry on Town

GRANTHAM FC finished the soccer season in May. The Midland League ended in January, with a new competition of eight clubs for the remaining four months.

## Keep it clean

SANITARY officer G L Robinson said the habit for butchers to hang meat outside their shops should be discouraged.

He said: "Dust is sure to blow on to it."

---

**TAILORED UNIFORMS for the SERVICES**

by GEORGE MILLS

Careful study of regulation details - fine materials - hand tailoring - and good, honest craftsmanship are the solid foundatios on which our reputation for military tailoring has been built.

In whichever Service you may be commissioned, we can supply you with expert advice to the last detail. Come and discuss your Service requirements with us.

TRENCH COATS, R.A.F. WATERPROOFS, SERVICE CAPS, SHIRTS, TIES, GLOVES, ETC. ALWAYS IN STOCK

Phone 302

**GEORGE MILLS Ltd**
Military and Civilian Tailors
**HIGH ST. - GRANTHAM**

# Grantham in the News — 1940

## Railway bridge targeted by dive bomber

SPITTLEGATE Hill railway bridge was hit by a high-explosive bomb only minutes after the Flying Scotsman had past beneath.

It was dropped by a Junkers Ju-88 which appeared out of the clouds at about 4.30pm and dropped two bombs.

Anti-aircraft guns failed to bring it down.

Minutes later, a dozen bombs fell at Stanton Ironworks' mines at Gunby.

Apart from damage to the bridge, six buildings were demolished and 86 were damaged.

Only one person was killed, a visitor who had left London to escape the air raids.

He was in an outdoor toilet behind South Parade where outbuildings appeared to have been sliced through like a knife. Nine other people were slightly injured.

One South Parade resident, Mrs Wright, whose son was on leave from the Navy said: "Strange things happened.

"Bricks were clattering behind the plaster and our crisp clean tablecloth was suddenly covered in black dust. My husband found the stairwell full of wood and debris."

*Some of the successful Boys Central pupils*

## Boys' struggle to save

PUPILS at the Boys' Central School, Sandon Road, completed their National Savings target in half the time planned.

They saved £1,000 in 26 weeks, a feat they expected to take a year.

They then went on to save £5,000 in the full year, much to the delight of headteacher Sammy Thorpe.

As part of the campaign, woodwork master Ben Sewell made a model Spitfire with a 4ft wing span which was parked at the main gate.

The scheme was called Mein Kamf - German for My Struggle - the title of Adolf Hitler's autobiography.

## I'll guide German planes says jailed blackout widow

A 64-year-old Colsterworth widow was the first person in the district to be prosecuted for a blackout offence.

She was sent to jail for one month by Spittlegate court for allowing light to escape from her house.

Special constable Cyril Wright, of Colsterworth, saw the light just before midnight.

He knocked on the door and the light was immediately extinguished. Constables Wright and Collingwood removed the light bulbs and electrical fuses, leaving her without lights.

Inspector Taylor said he visited the widow and asked for her assurance not show lights again.

She replied: "No! I shall not draw my blinds down.

"When the warning is sounded I shall put on all my lights to help the aeroplanes to come and destroy all this wickedness."

She was led from the courtroom muttering under her breath.

## Returning serviceman ordered from home

A SOLDIER returning from active service was told to quit his home because it was in his dead mother's name.

L Corp Robert Butler had lived with his parents at Porch Cottage, Harlaxton, all of his life.

But when his mother died, the owner, Miss Hattersley won a county court application for possession, as he was not the legal tenant.

Mr Butler, who served in Malta, Palestine and India, had married earlier in the year and his wife also lived at the cottage.

# 1941 Grantham in the News

## Man told to pay damages in breach of promise action

A 32-year-old Harlaxton man was ordered to pay £60 damages to a Holbeach girl in a breach of promise action.

The banns had been read, the ceremony arranged and the cars booked, when he called off the marriage.

The under sheriff told the court: "Misconduct between the couple had taken place. This has reduced the girl's chances considerably."

The former farmworker had left the land and was working in a factory for £2.70 per week.

---

**SIX SHIPS** are required to import the necessary raw materials for new tyres.

**ONE SHIP** only is required for necessary raw materials for Tyresoling an equal number of tyres.

**LEAVING FIVE SHIPS** free to import food, munitions and essential imports.

Here you see two Tyresoled tyres ready to give guaranteed new tyre milage over again at half cost. Every make and size can be Tyresoled. Large stocks also available from immediate fitting. Save for yourself and the Nation by fitting Tyresoles.

don't scrap smooth tyres - have them

# TYRESOLED

Local Tiresoles Factory

**NORTH ROAD GARAGE**
**GREAT PONTON**

---

## Bravery aboard a trawler

JACK Ashford (21), of Albert Street, Grantham, was awarded the Distinguished Service Medal for his part in bringing down two German planes as a gunner aboard Grimsby trawler Arctic Trapper.

The capable crew only used three shells to accomplish this feat.

The trawler was under machine-gun attack from the enemy bombers when its crew fired their first shell, which damaged two planes before two direct hits brought them down.

The Artic Trapper was lost two weeks later, although Mr Ashford was not aboard.

## All the King's men

A FARMWORKER walking across Caythorpe fields early in the morning, approached a stranger who demanded to know his business there at such an early hour.

The rustic said he was going to fetch the cows for milking.

After the man refused to allow him to go any further, a fight ensured and colleagues of the man restrained him.

It was then revealed they were from the secret service and were guarding the royal train in a nearby siding, where the King and Queen were sleeping.

# Grantham in the News — 1941

## Star Judy is a wow at home

THE Mayor's Emergency Fund was £57 the richer thanks to a personal appearance by Grantham-born superstar Judy Campbell.

Although the RAF dance band, led by Ronnie Aldrich, failed to appear due to the blackout, the daughter of cinema owner John Campbell was on stage at the Picture House.

Among her repertoire was a Nightingale Sang in Berkeley Square, backed by Grantham pianist Roy Farmer.

Of appearing in her own town she said: "I was petrified. In London if you flop you're with strangers.

"In Grantham I just had to be a success."

## Vicar's son saves planes

CAYTHORPE vicar's son Tom Ison displayed outstanding courage when he extinguished the flames of a burning aircraft in a hanger.

His actions probably saved other aircraft nearby.

He dashed through the fierce flames, his hands burned and his clothes on fire, to reach the petrol tap which he turned off.

His prompt action saved aircraft and components worth thousands of pounds.

Two men who had been working on the wings jumped clear.

Mr Ison said: "It was all over in a matter of seconds. I knew where the petrol tap was although it was red hot.

"I also kicked a bucket of inflammable liquid over to stop the flames from spreading."

*A gun crew at BMARCo's factory*

## Boss shoots down the bomber which killed 16

SIXTEEN workers were killed and 30 injured in an air raid on the Ministry of Aircraft Production factory, Springfield Road.

Another man died and eight were injured minutes earlier, when bombs fell in New Beacon Road.

The sirens sounded at about 2pm, half-an-hour before a Junkers Ju-88 appeared over Hall's Hill, shadowed by a pair of Hurricanes. It banked as it crossed the MAP factory next door to BMARCo.

Home Guard machine gunners on the roof fired into the low cloud where they heard, but could not see, the aircraft.

Managing director Denis Kendall was one of the gunners and claimed to have scored a fatal hit on the aircraft.

It dropped four bombs on the factory as the gunners opened fire, then disappeared over Hall's Hill with one engine blazing.

The first bomb landed near Buckminster Gardens damaging 237 buildings and leaving 88 people homeless. The second struck the joiners shop, rolling under a bench and failing to explode.

A third hit the factory causing extensive damage and the fourth hit an air raid shelter, killing two workers.

One worker said: "I heard the plane overhead and saw tracer bullets through the roof. We ran for cover but I didn't make it.

"There was a thunderous crash followed by an engulfing current of compressed air.

"I struggled but I could only go with it.

"Next thing I was on the floor covered with asbestos and rubble."

When he got up, he found twisted metal girders and injured workers tangled with dead bodies.

Mr Kendall organised the removal of the unexploded bomb for repair work to begin before the UXB team arrived.

The Junkers crashed near Boston, where the four-man crew was arrested. Its propeller was presented to the factory as a trophy.

# 1941 Grantham in the News

## Man is fined for flashing

FIRE watchers were surprised to see a light flashing from a house in Bridge End Road, believing it to be a spy signalling.

Police were called who twice witnessed it being flashed three times.

They knocked on the door and a 36-year-old man, worse for drink answered.

He admitted to town magistrates he had a torch in his hand but was not aware he was committing a blackout offence. He was fined £1.

**Outside the ARP Centre, Barrowby Road**

## ARP warden gets driving ban

GRANTHAM Air Raid Precautions (ARP) was looking for an extra driver after one of their members was banned.

He was fined £5 and banned from driving for a year for drink-driving at Great Casterton.

Rutland magistrates refused to take into account the need for a car both as a warden and as a builder.

The Grantham man said although admitting the charge, he didn't feel guilty.

He said: "I had only had two drinks of mild and a sandwich at Corby at 7pm. I had been on duty until 5am and had only two hours sleep."

## Inflated bangers fine

A GRANTHAM butcher was fined £15 for overcharging for his sausages.

George Shepherd, of Redcross Street, a partner in Amos and Shepherd, Watergate, was also ordered to pay £4.22 costs.

Grantham Magistrates heard that the maximum price for beef sausage was 1½p per kg and pork 2½p per kilo.

But he got into trouble when he charged a Denton housewife 3½p for pork ones. She claimed they were very red and believed they were beef.

Shepherd said they were pork and were 50 per cent meat compared to the Ministry's figure of 39 per cent.

## Blasted stupid!

A HOUGH-on-the-Hill man was fined £2 for keeping a mortar smoke bomb he found in a field instead of handing it over to the authorities.

---

### AN ANNOUNCEMENT BY
# FOSTER BROS. Ltd.
(Grantham)

## THE TOBACCO PEOPLE

9, HIGH STREET
54, HIGH STREET
4, WESTGATE
10, WHARF ROAD
163, DYSART ROAD

## TOBACCO DIFFICULTIES

There are TEN times the number of persons visiting our SHOPS for the purpose of purchasing Cigarettes and Tobacco than we can possibly supply.

If everyone would purchase from the Tobacconist of 12 months ago, very few difficulties would exist.

Will those perons who WERE Regular Customers at any of our Shops please continue to call.

In future at our 54, HIGH STREET, AND 19, WHARF ROAD Shops, MEN ONLY will be supplied.

# Grantham in the News — 1941

## Five killed as aircraft collide over Harlaxton

TWO RAF pilots and the three-man crew of a Luftwaffe Junkers Ju-88 were killed when their two planes collided over Harlaxton.

Inspector Tom Graham from Glasgow, and his pupil Cpl Edwards, of Doncaster, were circling the town in their Oxford trainer.

They had taken off from RAF Spitalgate.

As they flew over Harlaxton they were confronted by the German plane.

According to eye witnesses, there had been a burst of cannon fire before the two aircraft crashed into each other.

Police Sergeant Hempstead, who was on duty, recalled: "I heard a burst of cannon fire and dashed outside. I saw an aircraft on fire heading towards Nottingham.

"It then turned towards the town before crashing into a cornfield at the bend of Barrowby Low Road. There was a violent explosion."

Police searching the area found the body of a man in a flying suit with a parachute attached. He was wearing a Luftwaffe uniform.

He was later identified as Lt Hans Hahn of Luftwaffe Gruffe 1, an elite squadron of 20 planes.

The charred remains of two others were found in the wreckage. It is believed that Hahn had put out his navigation lights to mingle with the encircling British trainers, awaiting the chance to shoot one down at point-blank range.

Hahn was the pilot who unsuccessfully attacked a Beaufighter landing at Wellingore airfield in April.

The Beaufighter pilot was Sqd Ldr Guy Gibson who later led the Dam Busters raid.

## Rationing

MEMBERS of Grantham's ladies groups were told clothing coupons would be introduced to ration clothing.

A Board of Trade representative told them it would include knitting wool.

## Fined £2.50 for refusing medical

A CONSCIENTIOUS objector was fined £2.50 for refusing to attend a medical board.

He was also detained for not more than 14 days so he could be taken before the board.

The farmworker said: "I have no intention of joining the armed forces and in a free country I have the right to be wrong."

He said he would join up for non-combat duties.

But he refused to attend St John's Hall, Launder Terrace, Grantham, for a medical examination.

*PART of the parade through Grantham for War Weapons Week showing the representatives from the Corporation Farm, Marston*

## War Weapons Week raises over a quarter of a million

WAR Weapons Week in Grantham raised double its target, a massive £257,000.

That worked out at £13 a head of population and instead of the five bombers planned, the RAF was able to purchase 13.

Among the attractions were an international rugby match, a bridge building display and a huge procession through the town.

# 1941 Grantham in the News

## Call to book

AVELING Barford had a vacancy for a female book-keeper aged 25 to 50 at its Houghton Road offices.

The going rate was £2.25 for a 47-hour week.

## Town boys on farm

THE local branch of the National Farmers Union announced plans for Grantham boys to train for farm work.

The boys would work on farms approved by the War Agricultural Executive.

The 14 and 15-year-olds would receive 25p a week plus free board.

## Front page news

THE Grantham Journal front page carried news instead of advertisements for the first time since the paper was founded in 1854.

## High fliers

EMPLOYEES of Grantham Co-operative Society contributed £3,568 towards purchasing a Spitfire for the RAF.

Directors doubled the sum and a cheque for £7,136 was handed over to the Ministry of Aircraft Production.

## Blackout fine

THE manageress of Grantham Steam Laundry, Belton Lane, was fined £2 for Lighting Restriction Order offences.

The court was told seven windows and a fanlight were improperly screened.

**Ann Lamplugh Robinson demonstrates good vegetable growing**

## Insects are the fifth column says horticulturist.

DOZENS of would-be gardeners turned out for a demonstration of good vegetable growing practice on St Catherine's Road.

Ann Lamplugh Robinson of Plant Protection was at the Grantham war horticultural committee's demonstration plot near the river.

She showed how fertiliser is essential for maximum production and how to deal with garden pests.

She said: "Pests such as aphids and slugs are the fifth column of the garden. They must be eradicated."

## Farmer sick of apple thefts

AN Aveling Barford employee was fined £1.50 for stealing 2kg of apples worth 42p from an orchard at nearby Paper Mill Farm.

The owner, Richard Harris, of Huntingtower Road, said he was having considerable trouble from the factory workers on night shift.

He had been keeping surveillance in the early morning when he saw two men in his orchard.

He caught one man but the other escaped.

## Nurse awarded for bravery

NURSE Alice Rooke was awarded the BEM for heroism.

The former health visitor for Hough and Fulbeck worked through a bombing raid while injured and temporarily blinded by dust.

Miss Rooke also burrowed under rubble to rescue a buried girl.

## Just not cricket

A GERMAN bomber dropped four high-explosive bombs on Grantham.

They all fell harmlessly on the King's School cricket field, North Parade.

# Grantham in the News          1942

*Stuart Street after the air raid*

# Thirty-two killed and 500 homeless in October air raid

THIRTY-TWO people were killed and 41 injured – nearly half of them seriously - in an October air raid.

More than 600 properties were damaged, 20 demolished and 80 needed extensive repairs.

More than 500 people were left homeless.

The sirens sounded at 9.30pm when two German bombers were spotted. When the planes dropped flares, it was said to be like daytime.

Most of the casualties were in the Stuart Street area hit by two high-explosive bombs.

Several houses in Dudley Road and others in the Uplands Drive area were damaged by firepot incendiary bombs.

The first two high-explosive bombs were believed to be targeting Bomber Command HQ at St Vincent's but one fell in the road in Bridge Street and the other in Stuart Street.

The second was the more serious.

An air raid shelter in the street took a direct hit and was demolished together with a score of homes, killing 20 people.

The next batch fell in the Uplands Drive area, scoring direct hits on four Ermine Close homes.

An eye witness in Stuart Street said when emergency services arrived, the scene of devastation was bathed in the weird light of the moon.

He said: "Dust, glass and bricks were scattered randomly with bleeding, mutilated bodies, limbs no longer attached and unrecognisable pieces of human bodies lying everywhere.

"The air was rent with the cries and screams of the injured victims and the shouts of rescuers."

Builders were taken off the Beeden Park building site to dig extra graves for the casualties.

*Ermine Close*

# 1942 Grantham in the News

## No coupons

A NEWARK man was fined £5 by Grantham Magistrates for selling silk stockings to fellow employees.

He sold them to workmates at BMARCo, Springfield Road, without asking them to surrender their coupons.

Admitting selling £1.80 worth at the factory he insisted he did not make a penny profit.

## Engineer's death

ENGINEER Reginald Tite died after getting trapped by a pulley belt.

Mr Tite (50) had been repairing the belt at Grantham Steam Laundry, Belton Lane, while it was running and became trapped.

Eyewitness Violet Hoys said: "I saw him in the roof going round and round in the pulley."

## Gun law fine

A GRANTHAM youth was fined £2 by Borough Magistrates for carrying a seven-chamber 0.22 revolver to work.

He told the court he thought being a member of the Home Guard gave him the right to carry arms.

## Shop time

LUNCHTIME closing for the town's shops ended after the Chamber of Commerce agreed to a daily priority shopping hour between 12.15pm and 1.15pm..

This was for women working in factories.

## Family of five in one bed

A NINE-week-old baby who slept with four others, died of suffocation.

But the mum told an inquest, she had just bought a cot and was about to collect it.

The woman said she usually slept with the baby in her arms and three other children at their Uplands Drive home.

During the fatal night, she was awoken by one of them shouting that bombs were dropping.

She said: "I noticed blood around the baby's nose. It was then I realised the baby was dead."

The father told the inquest that although there was a spare bed but the family liked to be together during air raids.

He slept on the rug downstairs.

## Girls caught on airfield

TWO teenage girls were fined £1 each after being caught on an airfield without permission. They were spotted with a Polish airman going into a hangar at RAF Spitalgate.

The defendants said they only went in out of curiosity.

Pleading guilty, they said they thought it all right as they were with a member of the RAF. The airman was arrested and court marshalled.

One of the girls was fined a further 50p for failing to sign her identity card.

## Boon for working mums

GRANTHAM'S second nursery was opened in Wyndham Park.
It was to be similar to one on St Catherine's Road.

The paintwork was a 'restful' brown and cream and had ample facilities to wash children's towels and bedding, a kitchen and plenty of cupboards.

The babies' room had dropside cots and for older children, low tables and chairs.

There was a pram shelter with a weatherproof blind.

Children were taken between 7am and 7pm, but their mothers had to be employed.

## Well Saved

EARLESFIELD County School won the Kesteven Savings Shield with 98.7 per cent of pupils taking part.

Swaton CE School was runner up with 98 per cent.

---

**BOROUGH of GRANTHAM SALVAGE COMMITTEE**

## RAGS & BONES

are essential
to provide the
RAW MATERIALS
for
Munitions of War

Please Keep Rags as
Clean and Dry as
possible

SAVING SALVAGE
MEANS MORE
MUNITIONS

# Grantham in the News       1942

## Boy dies after being trapped by rail truck

A FOURTEEN-year-old Denton boy died in hospital after being trapped by the wheel of a railway truck.

Ronald Hubbard had been employed at Stanton Ironworks since leaving school the previous year.

His father and fellow-employee E H Hubbard told an inquest he had seen his son jump on to the wagons several times from the level crossing to go to the office where he worked.

He said he had warned him the area was slippery.

Engine driver G Renshaw, of Harston, said he saw Ronald as he passed.

The next minute his fireman said: "Hold on. He's under the van."

They had to reverse the engine to free his leg before moving him to a nearby hut for treatment.

Death was caused by lacerations, blood loss and shock.

*BMARCo workers get on with their job*

## Arms maker under fire

MUNITIONS company BMARCo was attacked by the Commons Public Accounts Committee for refusing to deliver arms until the price was fixed.

They said the company, run by local MP Denis Kendall, caused concern over its "persistant refusal to afford full access to its accounts and records."

They described this as "indefensible" and accused the company of profiteering during a time of war.

But an angry Mr Kendall told his constituents he had taken exception to the excessive publicity and had sent a telegram to Prime Minister Churchill about it.

## Denis wins the Grantham seat

SUPPORTERS of the Independent candidate Denis Kendall admitted they were surprised when he won the Grantham seat in a Parliamentary by-election.

In a straight fight against Air Chief Marshal Sir Arthur Longmore (National Government) he won with a 367 majority.

It was the first defeat for the National Government Party, formed at the outbreak of war. Managing director of arms manufacturer BMARCo, Mr Kendall, whose slogan was: "Production for victory" polled 11,758 votes against Sir Arthur's 11,391.

Mrs Violet Van der Elst, of Harlaxton Manor, due to be the third candidate, was too ill to travel from London on the day nominations closed. Mr Kendall covered the Grantham constituency by motorcycle during the campaign to cut down on petrol use.

The by-election was caused by the elevation to the peerage of sitting MP Sir Victor Warrender, who became Lord Bruntisfield.

The Conservatives had held the seat since 1923 when they took it from the Liberals.

## Six months at ninety-one

A 91-year-old man was sent to prison by Grantham Magistrates for obtaining £1.50 from a woman by false pretences.

Chairman of the bench Forsgate Weekley said: "You will be out of harm's way for six months."

# 1942 Grantham in the News

## Blaze wrecks pavilion

THE timber cricket pavilion on London Road was gutted in a mystery blaze.

The alarm was raised shortly after 8pm and the National Fire Service was on the scene within a minute closely followed by two more engines.

By then, the building was well ablaze.

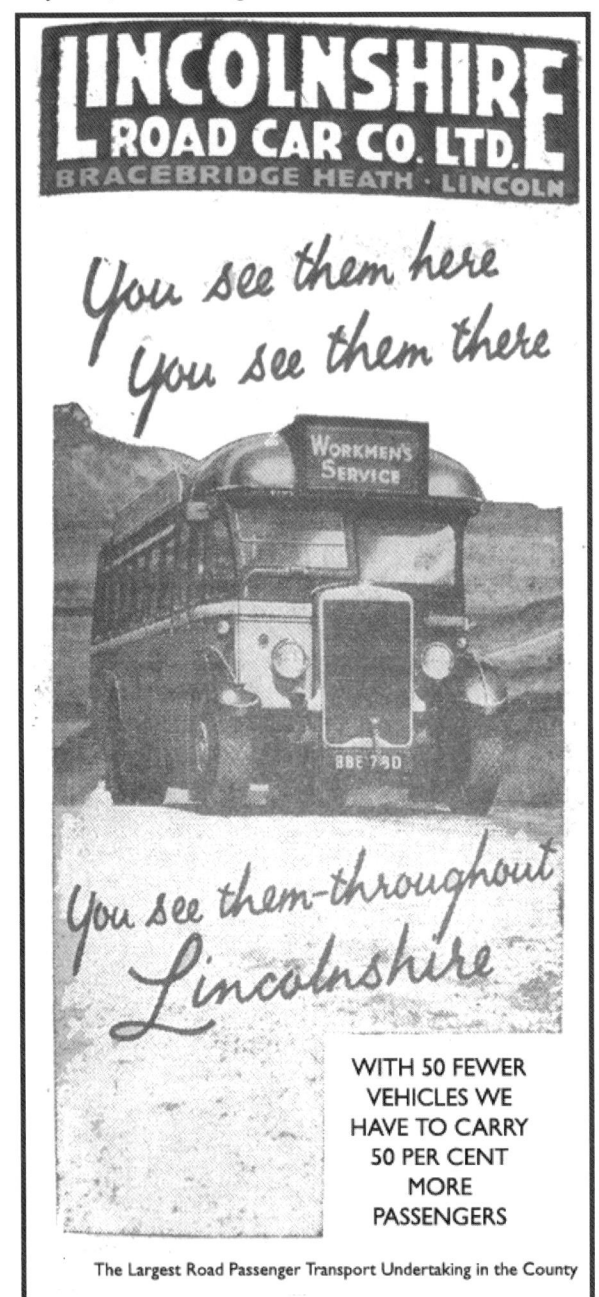

**LINCOLNSHIRE ROAD CAR CO. LTD.**
BRACEBRIDGE HEATH · LINCOLN

*You see them here
You see them there*

WORKMEN'S SERVICE

*You see them-throughout Lincolnshire*

WITH 50 FEWER VEHICLES WE HAVE TO CARRY 50 PER CENT MORE PASSENGERS

The Largest Road Passenger Transport Undertaking in the County

## Baby seen hanging from upper window

A FOUR-year-old girl holding on to the legs of a baby hanging head downwards from an upstairs window, shocked a crowd gathered in Kettle's Place, New Street.

It led to their mother being brought before the borough court for neglecting her five children, all under 16.

Mr W Hamilton, of the NSPCC, said the children were neglected, although were clean and well fed.

But the accused often left the children alone to do as they wished which led to this incident.

Pc How said he visited the home on one occasion to find a seven-year-old girl nursing a baby in front of an unguarded, blazing fire.

The mother was given a conditional discharge.

## Preacher jailed

A GRANTHAM man was sentenced to nine months jail with hard labour for refusing to take a medical.

The Ministry of Labour and National Service, prosecuting, told town magistrates the man had registered as a conscientious objector but had refused to attend two medicals.

The accused told the court his life's work was to preach the gospel and took a neutral stand as far as the war is concerned.

## Youth hit by warning shot

AN Air Ministry clerk was fined £1.75 for unlawfully wounding a 17-year-old youth at Foston.

The youth, who earlier that day had been found guilty with two friends of damaging a cherry tree, claimed he had been shot.

The clerk said he saw the youths breaking the branches to steal fruit, took an airgun from his car and fired a warning shot.

The youth claimed he was hit on the knee by a pellet and had to seek hospital treatment.

## Cheap grub

MAYOR of Grantham Benjamin Sindall praised the menu at Bjorlow's canteen.

On offer at the Earlesfield tannery were soup, roast beef, Yorkshire pudding, baked and roast potatoes with Brussels sprouts, and jam sponge - all for 4p.

# Grantham in the News — 1942

## Shock at slogans scrawled on boilers

SLOGANS inscribed on eight boilers in a Grantham factory, calculated to cause dissatisfaction among the workforce, led to an appearance in the Police Court of a 19-year-old youth from Inner Street.

Among the phrases used were: "Why waste steel on these", "Will these bring Rommel's defeat?", "Increase the bacon ration" and "Will these do any good for the second front?"

Det Officer Bramhall said the youth told him he had only done it for a joke and did not see any harm in it.

Pleading guilty, the youth begged for leniency.

The youth told the court he was hard working, putting in 59 hours a week.

He had applied to join the Royal Navy and was waiting for a vacancy.

Magistrate Forsgate Weekley said the court was entitled to take drastic action but, after deliberation, dismissed the case under the First Offenders Act.

He said the young man had just been very silly.

## Foreman did go to France

A FILM released during the year, The Foreman went to France, was based on the exploits of a Grantham man.

The film, written by J B Priestley, told how an Englishman crossed the Channel to retrieve vital machinery from under the noses of the occupying Germans.

After defying British red tape, he overcame dive-bombers, spies and roads clogged by refugees.

But Ted Carrick, played in the film by actor Clifford Evans, was in reality Melbourne Johns who went to France in 1940 to recover machinery for his employer BMARCo.

He was aided in the film by two soldiers played by Gordon Jackson and Tommy Trinder.

## Town de-railed for War Effort

IRON railings were stripped from St Peter's Hill, St Wulfram's churchyard and other civic buildings.

Metal posts, chains, bollards and gates were removed as part of the national effort to supply surplus metal to the iron and steel works.

More than 300 tonnes were removed from Grantham. After the railings around the green on St Peter's Hill were taken, notices were erected saying: "Keep off the grass".

Nearly 300 tonnes of scrap metal was collected.

From left are, back – C. Willers, A. Senior, E Morley, W. Beale, V. R. Waterhouse, A. R. Musson and L. Kellond; third row – W. Warren, W. G. Scudemore, S. Greetham, K. Whysall (pharmacist), W. Leeson, E. Goodley, A. Morris, W. Forth, J. C. Welbourne and photographer Walter Lee; second row – R. Jackson, A. Imber, G. S. Bird, M. Broughton (head warden), E. Dowsett, M. Lepper and R. J. Murray; front (messengers) H. Hind, B. Willoughby & Gordon Baxter

## Ready for your defence

THE wardens of D Division, Civil Defence, were based at the former Roman Catholic School, next door to St Mary's Rectory, Barrowby Road.

The Clarion Cafe was also based there.

The picture was taken in the garden of the priest's house, behind the parish rooms.

# 1942 Grantham in the News

## Bus drivers say they are driven to strike action

BUS drivers employed by Lincolnshire Road car walked out on strike over a pay dispute.

They were demanding an extra 0.8p per hour on top of their 7.1p an hour.

A shop steward said: "We have had no increase since the outbreak of war.

"Driving in the blackout is a great strain. Even farmworkers get 9p an hour."

He said the drivers had only one day off in seven and did not get overtime premium rates even on Sundays.

Army drivers were called in to run essential services.

## Took shortcut over railway

TWO Grantham men were each fined a £1 for using the railway as a shortcut.

John Meek, of Bridge End Road, and Wallace Benjamin, of Walton Gardens, both pleaded not guilty.

Prosecutor D H Donaldson, for railway operator LNER, said too many people were getting through a fence on Springfield Road, going behind the loco shed and crossing the marshalling yards to the footpath between Huntingtower Road and Station Road.

## Failed to take turn

A COMPANY director was fined £2 for refusing to take his turn on fire watch.

## Mobile theatre launched

A THEATRE on Wheels (Princess Helena Victoria entertainments van) to entertain troops in remote Lincolnshire sites, was handed over to Grantham YMCA.

The presentation was made by the Duchess of Portland outside the Guildhall.

The fund-raising was organised by Mrs de Paravicini, of Birkholme Manor, near Corby.

## Conscience money

LINCOLNSHIRE Road Car bus company received a typewritten note plus cash saying: "Conscience money for not having paid my fare 10 years ago."

## Flat top homes named

GRANTHAM Borough Council agreed the name of the flat-top houses estate being built near the Meres would be Beeden Park in memory of Alderman Harry Beeden.

Councillors were very enthusiastic about the 847-house estate although Ald Rothwell Lee said: "I wouldn't want to live in one myself."

## Special guests

PENSIONERS had a treat at their St Catherine's Road club when three guests attended.

They were, on the right, from left, Coun Alfred Roberts, Mrs Violet van der Elst and Grantham MP Denis Kendall.

## Flying boat tragedy

FORMER King's School pupil Flt Sgt E J Hewerdine, of Grantham, was a member of the crew, including the Duke of Kent, who lost their lives in a Sunderland flying boat when it crashed in north Scotland.

# Grantham in the News — 1943

## Blast! It's the wrong type of bomb!

AN ARP exercise in Commercial Road became the real thing when what was supposed to be a smoke bomb contained gas, causing coughing and sneezing fits.

Several people were affected and mock casualties became real ones in the early round of the regional ARP competition.

At one stage, smoke became concentrated in a cul-de-sac and a sudden gust of wind drew it into a bomb-damaged house.

Three people in the house were acting as casualties waiting to be rescued.

Ten people were affected by the gas, including members of the Civil Defence and householders in Commercial Road, Rycroft Street, Brewery Hill, London Road and College Street.

Training officer F Coulson said the wrong type of bomb had been supplied.

## Christmas at home

WITH travel restrictions tighter than ever in this, the fifth wartime Christmas, it was a stay-at-home holiday for most people.

At the hospital, nurses chatted to patients at their bedsides and formed small choirs around pianos to entertain them. The Salvation Army Band also attended.

Christmas dinner was goose, not turkey as the previous year, while at the County Institution, inmates enjoyed rabbit pie.

*Gracie Fields leaves the State cinema by the rear door*

## Massive crowds turn out to meet 'Our Gracie'

SINGING superstar Gracie Fields, recently returned from an American tour where she lived in Hollywood, sang her way to the hearts of thousands of Grantham people who gathered on St Peter's Hill to listen to her.

She had been invited to the State cinema to entertain factory workers where she entertained about 2,000 people.

Afterwards, she appeared at a window overlooking the Guildhall. Traffic was diverted to avoid the mass of people.

The gesture thrilled the crowd who heard her over loud speakers, which earlier had been used inside the cinema.

Denis Kendall, boss at BMARCo, was keen that as wide an audience as possible should hear her. Employees from Aveling Barford, Ruston and Hornsby, R H Neal, Bjorlow and BMARCo were invited to the show.

The film star was delighted when she was presented with a basket of fruit from BMARCo welfare department.

She gave Mr Kendall an orange, Mr Bradshaw an apple then threw another orange into the audience telling whoever caught it to auction it for the hospital.

Afterwards, Gracie, her fellow artistes, the Mayor, Coun Sarah Barnes and the Mayoress had lunch at BMARCo's canteen.

## Billiards on Sunday

GRANTHAM MP Denis Kendall asked Home Secretary Herbert Morrison to lift the ban on playing billiards on Sundays during wartime for the benefit of servicemen.

He said skating rinks, cinemas, football and golf were all right on Sundays – so why not billiards.

He said: "It would bring good cheer and mental diversion to members of the services."

Mr Morrison said he was sympathetic but couldn't justify making such a move which would be strongly resisted.

# 1943 Grantham in the News

## Pigged off

TWO Ingoldsby men were each fined £5 for killing a pig without a licence.

The owner had completed the necessary form but his accomplice had slaughtered the animal before the licence had been issued.

They said it had become urgent as they had no food left to feed it.

## Shirty regulators

DRAPER Edgar Joel Beevers was charged by the price regulation committee with imposing conditions on the sale of shirts by selling them in pairs.

Fellow drapers supported him saying hardly anyone bought them singly.

## Diluted beer

BLUE Ram landlord George Grayson was fined £25 with costs of up to £10 for watering the beer.

He denied the charge saying the beer tested was not for public consumption.

He said it was his customers' leftovers including shandy and mineral water which they left for him to feed his pigs.

## Healthy hotel

THE Earlesfield Hotel, Dysart Road, won the challenge cup for raising the most cash for Grantham Hospital through its collection box.

Customers collected a record £254, beating the previous best by £100.

## Biker MP hits the ground

GRANTHAM MP Denis Kendall was hurt after he came off his motorcycle, which he used to save petrol.

The accident happened as he left the Harlaxton Road football ground.

He was severely shocked and an X-ray revealed a broken rib caused when he hit the motorcycle's handlebars.

Against medical advice, he travelled to London the following day where he was admitted to the Worshipful Company of Clockmakers, which carried the freedom of the City of London.

## Killed by bird

EDITH Bolton, of Huntingtower Road, Grantham, died in her bath after being overcome by carbon monoxide fumes.

It was caused by a bird's nest being built in the flue pipe, preventing the harmful gases from escaping.

A gas company official warned householders to keep their domestic appliances in order during the labour shortage.

He said many of his staff were now serving in the armed forces.

## Humby is on the right lines

LITTLE Humby got a telephone thanks to Grantham MP Denis Kendall.

Villagers said it must be the last place in England not to be connected.

One said: "It's back to the stagecoach days here. Residents have to cycle or walk several miles to get a doctor while farmers chase around the countryside looking for a vet."

A farmer agreed that the first telephone could be installed in his house and it would be available to other villagers.

## Farmers call time on summer

COUNTY farmers opposed plans for double-summertime - putting the clocks forward by two hours instead of one.

George Jenkinson, of Old Somerby, said: "Townspeople seem to imagine putting the clocks forward an extra hour means hens will lay more eggs because there are more daylight hours.

"Well they don't!"

## UTILITY FURNITURE

Cammacks have Inspected Advance Models of Utility Furniture and have no hesitation in recommending them. Sometime they may be available for general distribution. At present only holders of Official Permits can obtain them.

Information will be readily given at Cammacks.

**REGISTER AT CAMMACKS TODAY**

AT THE SIGN OF THE CLOCK

**CAMMACKS Ltd**

WESTGATE    GRANTHAM

# Grantham in the News — 1943

## Russian Flag taken from the Guildhall

THE hammer and sickle flag which flew from the Guildhall to mark the second anniversary of Russia entering the war, was taken down by pranksters.

It was recovered before the weekend and returned to its rightful place.

Dr Osiakovski, chairman of the of the Anglo-Soviet Friendship committee fumed afterwards: "You will not find any hooligans who try to steal British flags from Soviet buildings, going unpunished."

**Right: The Hammer and Sickle flies from the Guildhall**

## Campaigner sworn to secrecy over killers' medical records

ANTI-capital punishment campaigner Mrs Violet Van der Elst, of Grantham Castle (later Harlaxton Manor), was fined £10 by Bow Street Magistrates.

She was found guilty of contravening the Official Secrets Act over medical reports on persons who had been hanged for murder at Wandsworth Prison.

A sales manager for a photographic manufacturer said he went to her home in Addison Road, West London.

There Mrs Van der Elst's secretary produced 11 files and asked for a quotation to photograph the contents.

She said the papers had cost her £12 and she wanted them copied secretly.

The papers were hospital case notes on condemned people in Wandsworth Prison.

They gave details of their health, conduct and post-mortem examination results.

The man informed police and they were confiscated. Mrs Van der Elst refused to disclose the source of the documents

The accused said she was intensely patriotic and denied having paid for the documents.

Mrs Van der Elst was also ordered to give an undertaking she would not divulge the contents of the papers.

## Costly prank on teacher

TWO youths aged 14 and 17 were fined 25p and £1.15 respectively by Spittlegate magistrates for annoying a Hough-on-the-Hill teacher Eleanor Daft.

Miss Daft answered a knock on her back door and when she opened it, she was showered by a can of water propped above it. Both boys pleaded guilty to annoying Miss Daft.

## Vandals on Boxing Day

TUBS containing trees around Sir Isaac Newton's statue were overturned and a rhododendron bush stolen from the Guildhall as vandals struck on Boxing Day.

Parks and recreation chairman Ald Richard Brittain told councillors work to beautify the town was threatened by mischief. He said he hoped the ratepayers would bring the guilty to justice.

He said Wyndham Park had also been attacked, with broken glass, noticeboards wrecked and wallflower plants uprooted.

Ald Brittain said: "This has come at a time when a special effort is being made to enhance the beauty of Grantham."

## Park for potatoes

PART of Wyndham Park was ploughed up to grow potatoes.

The two acres south of the main playing field was to be restored once the war was won.

# 1943 Grantham in the News

## Youngest alderman appointed

COUNCILLOR Alfred Roberts was elected to the town's aldermanic bench, filling the vacancy left by Ald Holmes.

A native of Ringstead, Northamptonshire, Mr Roberts came to Grantham in 1913 as an assistant at Ald Clifford's Market Place grocery shop.

Five months later he was appointed manager of the London Road branch.

He volunteered for the Army in 1915 but was turned down on medical grounds.

In 1919, Mr Roberts bought the business on the corner of North Parade and Broad Street, from Thomas Parker who had run the shop for 49 years.

## Pony driver trapped for having no licence

CHRISTA Kerr, of Great Gonerby, was fined 37½p for driving a pony cart without a licence.

She told Pc McNeil she had owned the trap a month but was unaware a licence was required.

Supt A Dodson told Spittlegate magistrates: "We are going back to the Stone Age.

## Park for potatoes

PART of Wyndham Park was ploughed up to grow potatoes.

The two acres south of the main playing field was to be restored once the war was won.

## Roller out of control

A STEAMROLLER ran out of control along Station Road, Billingborough.

It was being towed by another steamroller when it gained momentum and began to overtake. As it drew level, the tow chain snapped.

Luckily, it came to a halt before the road junction where cyclists were enjoying themselves unaware of the danger.

## New YMCA centre

THE YMCA opened a youth centre on the two upper floors of a building on the west side of the Market Place.

It was open to young men aged 14 to 20 keen to work on pre-service work such as messengers for the Civil Defence.

## Drunken soldier went berserk

A NINETEEN-year-old Grantham soldier went berserk when arrested by police and had to be handcuffed. He was fined 50p plus 20p by Grantham magistrates for breaking a window in a police cell.

Dr Robbs, who was called to bring the prisoner round after he collapsed, said: "he became very violent and fought, kicked and scratched like a madman."

## Driven off the road

A 14-year-old from Barrowby was fined £1.50 and his farmer boss £2.50 for driving a tractor while aged under 17. Magistrates said they were being lenient as he did not go on the public highway.

**Opticians**
*Recognised by the Ophthalmic Benefit Approved Committee for*
NATIONAL HEALTH INSURANCE
**Rowley & Co**
72 HIGH STREET - GRANTHAM
Phone: 687 - facing Angel & Royal

# Grantham in the News — 1943

## Woman sought sack by sabotaging ammo

A PROBE into the mental status of a 24-year-old woman was ordered after she deliberately assemble shells wrongly.

The woman, who lived in Bourne, worked at a Grantham munitions factory.

She was charged with committing an act with intent to impair the efficiency of apparatus untended to be used by HM Services.

She admitted that she made up shell fuses wrongly although she had been taught the correct way.

She said she did it deliberately in order to be dismissed or moved to another department as she disliked the work.

She said: "I don't like the job. Other girls can chose their jobs. Why should I be pushed around?"

She was remanded in custody pending further investigations.

## Light work fine

A 64-year-old night-watchman was fined £2 for allowing a light to show from a canteen at the factory where he worked.

Ernest Browett, of Button Factory Lane (later Willow Lane), Harlaxton Road, Grantham, said he went on his rounds at 9pm and was certain no lights were showing then.

## Land girl knocked village postman off his bike

A MEMBER of the Women's Land Army was fined £3 with 35p costs after knocking a postman off his bike.

Doris Burgoyne, of Honington hostel, denied the charge but admitted one of failing to give her name and address to a constable and of failing to report an accident.

She was found guilty on both counts.

Auxilliary postman Cecil Drury said he was riding his bicycle towards Barkston station when he heard a motor horn behind. He drew to his left but was knocked to the ground receiving bruises.

## On the right lines

GRANTHAM railway station had loud speakers installed for the convenience of passengers.

Female announcers were trained and worked from a soundproof kiosk.

They gave bulletins of arrivals, departures and advice on labelling luggage, the importance of avoiding careless talk and other matters of interest.

## Fuse mistake

JAMES Deeweet, of Harrowby Lane, was fined £1.50 for showing a light in his garage.

He told magistrates his maid had put a bulb in the socket and fused the light.

He said: "When I fixed the fuse the light went on without my knowledge."

The bench told him to be more careful in future.

## Fell from train

A SOLDIER who awoke on a moving train thought he had reached his destination, an inquest was told.

L/cpl Harold Lamb (38) of Albert Street, Grantham, opened the door and stepped out with his kit bag as the train sped along near Hereford.

He was returning from leave when the accident happened.

In civilian life, he worked at Aveling Barford and was a pianist with Reg Leachman's dance band.

---

**Henry Burton & Co.**

(GEO FOSTER)

Colliery Agents & Coal Merchants

GRANTHAM AND GREAT GONERBY

-----

DEPOT, GRANTHAM WHARF

---

Tel. 72.    Terms: Cash

**HALL & Co.**

WINE & SPIRIT MERCHANTS

All the best brands of SCOTCH and IRISH WHISKEY, BRANDY, GIN, RUN etc.' PORT, SHERRY, CLARET.

*42 High St., Grantham.*

# 1943 Grantham in the News

## Cinema owner and three managers fined

CINEMA owner and local councillor John Arthur Campbell was fined £3 by Borough Magistrates.

He admitted allowing people to stand in gangways at the Picture House, St Peter's Hill, Empire Theatre, George Street, and the Central Cinema, High Street.

Managers Thomas Hallam, Gloria Beck and Lionel Pinchbeck were fined £1 each for aiding and abetting.

Chief Constable Weatherhogg said the proceedings were taken under the Cinematograph Act Regulations which said gangways, staircases and passages leading to exits must be kept clear of obstructions.

Inspector Curry said in company with Sgt Hempstead he visited the Picture House.

There were 73 people standing and no exits except the entrance door.

Later at the Central, he saw a dozen people in the entrance hall.

Mr Curry said: "In the space between the two exit doors at the back downstairs I saw 22 persons standing. It was not possible to pass them unless they moved."

On his visit to the Theatre Royal he found no 'house full' notice.

He found 84 standing on the balcony with a further eight downstairs.

## Give your sons a good hiding says magistrate

THE fathers of two boys, aged 11 and 12, were each fined 50p after their sons admitted causing damage at the State Cinema.

The youngsters slashed the elbow rests and extracted sorbo rubber from them. Chief Constable Wetherhogg said this had been an ongoing problem and at last the perpetrators had been caught.

Manager Harry Sanders said: "We intend to prosecute in every case. Three weeks ago a wash-basin was smashed."

Magistrate E S Dunkerton said the boys required a good hiding from their fathers.

## Not for two

FRANCIS Harry Baldwin was fined 25p by Spittlegate Magistrates for carrying a second person on his bicycle.

## Mother-of-eight on theft charge

A MOTHER-of-eight was fined £1 for stealing a half-pint tumbler from the Nag's Head pub, Wharf Road.

The value was put at 10p.

She was rumbled when she asked the landlady for a second half-pint of mild without producing the glass in which the first one was served.

Landlady Gladys Horwill recovered the glass from the accused's handbag.

## Bandsman too tired

A FITTER employed by BMARCo was fined £10 by Grantham Magistrates for two offences of absenteeism and a further £10 for lateness.

He was charged by the Ministry of Labour and National Service under the Essential Work Order.

The accused played in a dance band three nights each week.

## Youngsters get the Blues

MEMBERS of the Grantham 47F Air Training Corps and the Girls Venture Corps combined to put on a show called Blue, White and RAF Blue.

While the Girls Venture Corps was separate, they occasionally collaborated for a show.

Grantham's ATC was one of the first 50 to be formed, in February 1941, taking over from the Air Defence Cadet Corps.

They met in the house next door to the post office on St Peter's Hill.

# Grantham in the News — 1944

## Yanks make Grantham's streets unsafe for women claims MP

AMERICAN troops made life intolerable for Grantham women, Grantham MP Denis Kendall told Parliament.

He said: "I have evidence that it is unfit for a woman to walk unescorted through the town either at night or in daytime."

The statement caused uproar in the House although he received support from local women's organisations, who demanded more women constables.

A joint statement issued by the Mayor Alfred Barnett, Ald Rothwell Lee and Lord Brownlow said they had no evidence whatsoever of any incidents which supported the "grave and reckless" charges made by their MP.

The Chief Constable of Grantham said he had received no complaints but Mr Kendall was adamant.

"The United States authorities are failing to assist to its utmost in disciplining its troops," he told the shocked House.

"But we are more anxious to extend the hospitality to the US troops for whom I have a wholehearted affection."

Fighting against cries of "withdraw" from all sides of the chamber, Mr Kendall insisted he had evidence in letters from married and single women as well as the church in Grantham.

Canon Harold Leeke, the vicar of St Wulfram's, saw the problem as one of litter.

He said: "The point is contraceptive appliances should not be left in public because that is poisoning innocent minds.

"Situations have arisen whereby children are in danger of disease."

Mrs Ayres of the Salvation Army said women were equally to blame. She called for more policewomen to be appointed.

The Americans had arrived six months earlier at Barkston Heath.

They also took over St Vincent's, following the departure of no 15

**Denis Kendall**

Group Bomber Command and were billeted at Shirley Croft, Harrowby Road.

Altogether 30,000 GIs were in the Grantham area.

With sweets and nylons the GIs won the hearts of local girls causing friction with many of the town's young men.

## Fireman killed while adjusting blackout

GRANTHAM fireman Harry Sharlow was killed between King's Cross and London while adjusting the blackout on his locomotive.

Mr Sharlow, of Dysart Road, was struck by a bridge at Woolmer Green, Hertfordshire.

Driver Horace Healey, of Houghton Road, said as they approached Welwyn, he looked round and saw Mr Sharlow who was lying on the footplate with severe head injuries.

Marks were found on a bridge which suggested that was the cause of the accident.

The coroner at the Welwyn inquest recorded death by misadventure.

Mr Sharlow left a wife and nine-week-old daughter. He had played football for Grantham St John's and had trials with Grantham Town and Mansfield.

## Shotgun accident

JOHN Frederick Foster (77) of New Street, Grantham, was found dead at his home, with extensive gunshot wounds.

Sgt Ledger found the body between a table and the wall, with a double-barrelled hammer gun and his cycle on top of him.

An inquest said the accident happened as Mr Foster strapped the gun to his bicycle before going out to shoot vermin as he did most Sundays.

# 1944 Grantham in the News

## Three months on run

STANLEY Curry, of Uplands Drive, a prisoner-of-war in Italy, was transferred to Germany.

The former council worker had escaped and was at large for three months but was recaptured after falling ill.

## Two for the top

MADELIN Edwards and Margaret Roberts were appointed joint head girls of Kesteven and Grantham Girls' School.

It was the first time the distinction was shared.

Miss Roberts was the daughter of Ald Alfred Roberts.

## Journal fined

THE Grantham Journal was fined £1 for allowing a light to be shown during blackout hours.

The light came from three large windows in the firm's machine room.

## Orange disorder

ABOUT half of the oranges which arrived in Grantham were rotten.

In one case, there were only 12 edible ones in a batch of 150.

The long delay in storage and transit plus exposure to frost, were blamed.

## Film star at Belton

SCREEN idol Captain Clark Gable was guest of Lord and Lady Brownlow at Belton House, in July.

Afterwards he met Grantham MP Denis Kendall.

## Guildhall to be open to all

THE Guildhall was thrown open to the public again after being kept exclusive.

It followed the maiden speech by new town councillor Susan Brace, who claimed Grantham was becoming unsociable to visitors.

She said: "I honestly believe we are in danger of becoming a one horse town - the lowest form of community."

Her remarks followed claims that two American servicemen, turned up at a Guildhall dance, but were told they must sit still and listen to the band for 25p each.

She said: "I think that is a frightful reflection on our hospitality."

The town council agreed to throw the Guildhall open to everyone, including British servicemen and Allied troops.

## Pubs must stay open says bench

FORTY-six of Grantham's 78 publicans were put on probation by magistrates for failing to keep open during the amended hours agreed in October 1942.

But the landlords questioned why they should remain open during the permitted hours when they had nothing left to sell, especially as they would be wasting electricity by doing so.

Magistrates said that if everyone didn't open from 8pm-10pm then the pubs that did would be overcrowded.

The Brewster sessions overturned the decision at a later hearing.

## Casting new light wartime gloom

GRANTHAM people had their biggest surprise of the war when new street lights were erected.

Coun Benjamin Sindall, chairman of the lighting committee, said 250 of the old 'starlight' gas lamps were being replaced by the improved 'moonlight' lamp. He claimed these would be brighter.

He said "The new system will be just as economical as the previous star lighting so far as gas consumption is concerned and the lighting will be infinitely better.

"It is doubtful whether we shall resume normal street lighting for a time because of the shortage of coal."

---

**SHARP & SONS**

THE MUSIC SHOP IN GRANTHAM

MUSIC - RADIO - RECORDS - PIANOS
AND ALL MUSICAL INSTRUMENTS

QUALITY REPAIRS
Estimate Free

15 FINKIN STREET :: GRANTHAM

# Grantham in the News — 1944

## Women preyed on American servicemen

THREE women who went on the streets of Grantham looking for victims, were jailed for stealing from American servicemen and trespassing on military premises.

They picked up soldiers, sometimes spent the night with them, then picked their pockets.

A 19-year-old of Harlaxton Road pleaded guilty to stealing a wallet containing £9.50, another containing £1.50 and a watch worth £15 from three members of the USAAF.

She was jailed for three months on each of the four charges.

The second woman, a 19-year-old from Uplands Drive, was jailed for two months after spending the night in a corporal's bed.

The third woman, who live at Castle Bytham, was jailed for four months for stealing a wallet containing £8 from a USAAF serviceman at the Golden Fleece pub, Grantham.

She admitted she did it while the soldier was kissing her.

She was jailed for a further month for committing an act contrary to public decency and propriety in the shelters in Grantham bus station.

## Reds go local

THE Grantham branch of the Communist Party decided to take an increased interest in local government by setting up ward groups.

Secretary Mr A G Jenkins said it was brought about by the conduct of the town's affairs and because of the party's dissatisfaction with the ruling parties.

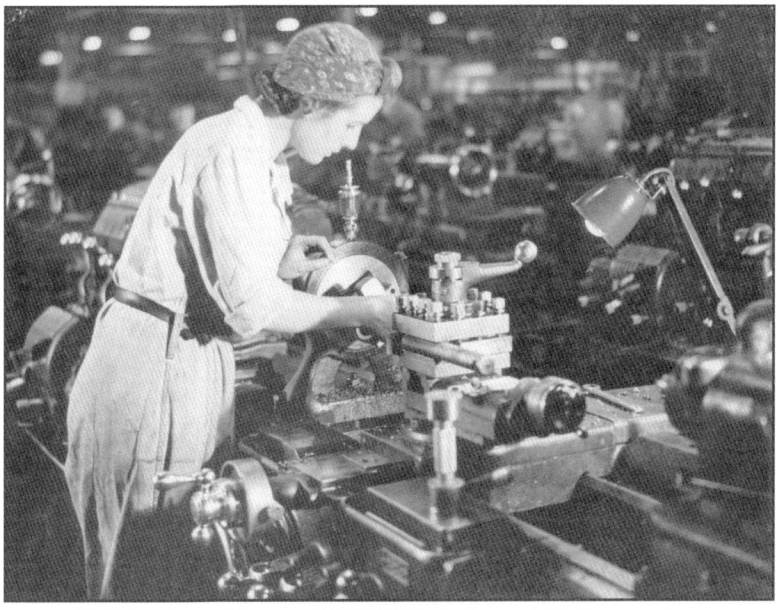

*Safety of machinery at BMARCo is brought into question*

## BMARCo fined after woman worker loses an ear

MUNITIONS maker BMARCo, of Springfield Road, was fined £25 for failing to fence off part of an automatic lathe.

It led to operator Hazel Stephen catching her hair in the machine removing her scalp and right ear.

The company was fined a further £30 for three similar offences.

Mr R Varley for the company said if the machine's had no gap above the guard it would not be possible to operate.

He said no one could fall accidentally against the machines, it was due to the complacency of operators.

He said: "The girl, who had worked on the machine for three years, leaned over and caught her hair.

"She had probably become so used to the machinery, and having no accident before, had come to look upon the danger with a certain degree of contempt."

## Call to ban tax free Irish from land jobs

IRISH workers should be banned from the land in England unless they remain in the country for at least eight months, members of Grantham NFU agreed.

It followed talks with the Inland Revenue over the method of taxing the income of the Irish workers, which was unjust to their English counterparts.

Those spending less than six months in the UK did not have to pay British income tax.

MP Denis Kendall said farmers should not employ Irish workers unless they are paid the same as Englishmen.

# 1944 Grantham in the News

## Grief for WAAF

A YOUNG Grantham WAAF was told her fiance had been killed the day before they were due to marry.

Betty Coleman (20), one of six daughters of Mr and Mrs T Coleman, of Oxford Street, was set to marry Flt Sgt pilot Jack Newman, of Oxford.

But days before he was killed on flying duties.

The couple had been trying to name the day for the past six months, but his RAF duties kept intervening.

## Plans for peacetime

IMPORTANT post-war developments and extensions at Aveling Barford's Invicta Works, Houghton Road, were outlined in plans put before the town council.

Paper Mill Lane, which split the factory in two, was a serious handicap to expansion and the company asked for it to be stopped up from the factory perimeter southwards.

The company also asked for the footpath from Paper Mill Lane, which crossed the LNER main line, to be closed.

## Children went on wrecking spree

SIX children aged eight to 10 smashed 1,104 drainpipes, totalling 350m in length, at Harrowby Land Settlements.

Each of their parents was fined £1 by Grantham Juvenile Court.

Magistrate Dr Charles Frier told the children that it was not nice to smash things up.

"How would you like someone to break all your toys?" he asked them.

## Phone call by Beeden Park

AN angry Beechcroft Road resident said the new Beeden Park estate, in Grantham, was being held back by the GPO.

Mr F Mattinson said he had written to the head postmaster who informed him there were no plans for a phone box at the new estate.

Mr Mattinson said: "There are 700 new residents up here. In the town centre, there are two kiosks at the bus station and one across the road at the post office as well as a phone inside.

"When people moved to this estate they have the right to phone the doctor etc.

"They spend plenty of money beautifying the estate with trees but what we need is a public phone."

A GPO spokesman said it was not appropriate at this time.

## Boy dies of tetanus

A TEN-year-old Hull evacuee died after slicing his hand in a chaff-cutter at Aslackby.

Brian Henson, who had moved to the village in 1940, cried: "I have cut my finger off."

Horseman Harry Hildred, with whom Brian lodged, said the farmer's wife Mr Walker bandaged his hand and summoned Dr Holms.

The right thumb was partly severed and his index finger slit with many lacerations on the tissues.

Although considerable serum was used, they were unable to stop his death from tetanus an inquest in the death was told.

## Demob batman to sweep chimney - MP

GRANTHAM MP Denis Kendall called on the Army to release a Grantham chimney sweep from batman duties saying his trade was more important than cleaning officer's brasses.

**HOME AGAIN**

From the ends of the earth, even in war-time, MARSDENS bring to you a wonderful range of PURE FRESH WHOLESOME FOODS

Over 70 Branches!

THERE'S A BRANCH NEAR YOU

**MARSDENS**

GROCERS FOR 'THE QUALITY'

# Grantham in the News — 1944

## Long queues for children's hour

THE introduction of Children's Hour by London Road confectioners F W Pulford proved a big hit with youngsters.

The shop, near the Cambridge Street junction, set aside 60 minutes a week for the children to spent their coupon allocation.

Queues several deep stretched along London Road.

## Shot down bomber just misses a farmhouse

A STIRLING Bomber was shot down and crashed at Hill Top Farm, Caythorpe,

The crew were from No 1654 Heavy Bomber Conversion unit based at RAF Wigsley, five miles west of Lincoln.

Pilot Flt Sgt Joseph Nicholson of the RAFVR and his crew of seven had taken off from their base for a long night cross-country exercise, combined with bombing practice over the ranges at Bassingham. While in the range area, it was intercepted and shot down in the early hours by an enemy intruder, believed to be a Messerschmitt BF 410.

The German pilot claiming the kill was Hpt Dietrich Puttfarken.

Four of the crew of the stricken bomber managed to bail out but four perished when the aircraft came down close to the farm on Caythorpe Heath.

Farmer Charles Theaker witnessed the aircraft being attacked and believed the bomber was steered away from his farmhouse at the last possible moment.

But part of the aircraft's undercarriage landed in the farm yard where several livestock, including the prize milker were killed. A fuel tank landed by the front door of the farmhouse. The wreckage was later cleared by Polish soldiers.

## Land for public use

A PIECE of land owned by Mrs G H Schwind was offered to the town council for the community.

The area of land, known as Colonel Parker's paddock, between St Catherine's Road and Avenue Road (later Stonebridge Road), measured about one hectare.

She gave it on condition it was used only as an open public space.

## Decorated by Monty

GRANTHAM soldier Lt John Pacey was decorated on the field of battle by Field Marshal Bernard Montgomery.

Mr Pacey, of High Street, was awarded the Military Cross for gallant and brave action on night patrol.

Twice wounded, he and his men silenced a German machine-gun post.

The former King's School pupil, who was in Galmancha, Normandy, at the time of the D-Day landings, was hit twice as he and his platoon approached their objective.

He continued, killing all the enemy gunners.

## Rosy future

FIFTEEN tonnes of rosehips were needed by the town to make rosehip syrup for children. The public was asked to gather them from gardens and hedgerows.

People taking firm, coloured rosehips to seed merchants Charles Sharpe, of Market Place, Grantham, were paid 2p per kilo.

# 1944 Grantham in the News

## Home Guard fined

A MEMBER of the Home Guard was fined £2 by borough magistrates for failing to attend a parade at Grantham gasworks.

He claimed he was sick and was certified, but magistrates heard he still went to work.

## Snowfall

THIRTY centimetres of snow fell in Grantham in April, a total of nearly 5,000 tonnes. Italian prisoners of war were employed to clear it up.

## Guide boss drops in

THE Chief Guide, Lady Baden-Powell, visited Grantham where she was guest of honour at a rally at Elsham House, home of district commissioner Lady Longmore.

## Driving to drink

THOMAS Pestell, of Victoria Street, was fined £2 by Spittlegate magistrates for driving to a village pub for a pint. He admitted misusing petrol by driving to the Gregory Arms, Harlaxton, other than on business.

## Rescued

TWO babies were passed through a first-floor window and six adults escaped by ladder, from a blazing house on North Parade.

One room was gutted and flames were spreading up the stairs when the alarm was raised.

A fireman rescued £50 in notes which had been left in a chair.

## Civil Defence on duty at Guildhall

TAKEN outside the garages at the Guildhall, these are members of the Civil Defence in Grantham.

Among them is the Rev E E Jourdain, a bachelor who was curate at St John's Church until 1950 when he succeeded the Rev Edwin 'Monkey' Millard as Vicar of St Anne's

## Sharp practice by razor market trader

A MARKET trader from Bradford was fined £21 with £21 costs by Grantham Magistrates for breaking the Provision of Goods and Services Act. On Grantham market, he sold a Gillette razor blade for 1½p instead of the regulation price of 1p.

Inspector Mrs Andrews was making test purchases at the market following complaints from the Chief Constable about overcharging.

The matter was dealt with by the price regulation committee.

Its investigations revealed the defendant had bought the blades from Petticoat Lane, London, for only 6p a dozen.

## Save scrap and win war says councillor

COUN George Mills, chairman of the borough salvage committee, said the public must fight against complacency.

He said salvage - especially paper, rags and bones - was still a war-winning weapon.

He told the WVS salvage stewards: "It's a wrong attitude for people to feel we are about at the end of the war.

"Four hundred components in a bomber are made of paper and we need to build 1,000 bombers."

He said putting rags, bones and paper in dustbins was defeating the war effort.

"It is also a criminal offence," he added.

# Grantham in the News  1945

## Population to double

GRANTHAM'S population was expected to grow to 50,000, according to a 20-year plan drawn up by the town and country planning committee.

The report, put before the borough council, dealt with the re-planning of 'Greater Grantham'.

It said the first five years would concentrate on housing arising from the lack of building during the war.

Expansion by the growth of new industry was the theme for the following 10 years.

The final five years would look at other needs including a civic centre. It was estimated that the town would need 2,000 new homes in the next 10 years.

Schemes already in hand included 100 pre-fabs off Belton Avenue, 180 houses on New Beacon Road, and 150 in the Harrowby Lane area.

The committee said it was alive to the importance of a civil airport for the town and district, by converting one of the aerodromes RAF Harlaxton, Gorse Lane, being preferred to RAF Spitalgate.

Watergate would be widened and a well-designed shopping centre developed.

A modern covered swimming pool was considered urgent.

The arrangement of market stalls in Market Place and Westgate, was thought to be undesirable and a covered market-hall would be built to accommodate them.

A covered arcade with shops lining it was to be formed from Westgate Hall to High Street. A substantial public hall for dances, concerts and meetings was also proposed.

**Children and their parents await the celebrations on St Peter's Hill**

## Big crowds turn out to cheer the end of war

CROWDS turned out on the streets to celebrate that peace had returned to Europe.

After six years of bloody conflict, during which Grantham became one of the most bombed towns for its size in England, the Nazis finally surrendered to the Allies.

VE Day, May 8, was declared a public holiday and although the metaphoric storm clouds had been lifted, real ones threatened to dampen celebrations. Fortunately the rain held back.

The bells of St Wulfram's could not ring out, as they had been taken down for repair the previous December.

Celebrations began in the afternoon with a united service conducted from the steps of the Guildhall, with thousands of people turning out.

Streets were alive with coloured bunting and national flags including the Stars and Stripes and the Hammer and Sickle.

Bands played in both Dysart and Wyndham parks.

A number of bonfires were lit in the town.

Even at midnight, in front of the floodlit Guildhall, people were singing, dancing and enjoying the new found peace.

Canadians, Americans, paratroopers and WAAFs joined civilians for the most exciting night anyone could remember.

## Stand down

MAGISTRATES refused permission for the State Cinema, St Peter's Hill, to allow 200 of its patrons to stand.

On safety grounds they would only allow 96 downstairs and none in the balcony.

# 1945 Grantham in the News

## Trombone mystery is solved at last

THE mystery of a trombone handed in to police after VE night celebrations was solved.

William Round, of Albion Terrace, said he had permission to use it to raise funds for the hospital. He made £2.19.

Mr Round said he had no idea how or where he lost it.

He said: "I also lost my best trilby hat."

An Army captain was seen playing the instrument at one stage, reportedly blowing so vigorously, he almost lost his false teeth.

## What a burn up!

CHILDREN in Gorse Rise spent the morning of VE Day making an effigy of Herman Goering by stuffing rags and paper into an old garment.

It was ceremonially burned after Prime Minister Winston Churchill's speech that afternoon.

## George Cross won by Great Humby hero

A GREAT Humby man who saved lives of both comrades and civilians was awarded a posthumous George Cross for his gallantry.

Signalman Kenneth Smith (24) of the RCS received the highest award in non-combat.

Among the letters to his mother, was one from the King saying "We pray that your country's gratitude for life so nobly given in its service may bring you some measure of consolation."

Mr Smith was a member of a patrol on the Adriatic island of Ist being attacked by saboteurs who laid time bombs in vital houses.

He had entered a house, where there were a number of partisans including children, as well as British troops were billeted, when he spotted a ticking bomb.

He picked it up and took it outside where it exploded.

Lieut Col Lloyd Owen said afterwards: "He saved the lives of many people and I cannot too highly express my admiration for his gallant action."

## Landslide for Denis

GRANTHAM MP Denis Kendall was returned to Parliament with a huge majority.

As the country as a whole swung towards Labour, the Independent's majority rose from 367 in 1942 to 15,513.

He polled 27,719 votes to Tory Sqd Ldr G A Worth's 12,206 and Labour's T S Bavin who received 7,728.

The 47,653 turnout was the biggest for many years.

## Alf takes the robes

ALDERMAN Alfred Roberts was chosen to take over as Mayor of Grantham in November.

He had been offered the post five years previously but declined.

He said: "I had to refuse last time. This time I felt it was due to the town and myself to accept."

Mr Roberts was a stalwart of Finkin Street Methodist Church.

He had been a local preacher for more than 20 years and a trustee of about 10 churches in the circuit.

A former chorister, he was secretary of the Methodist Guild, society steward, circuit steward and Sunday School secretary.

A grocer, Mr Roberts and his wife had two daughters. Muriel, a physiotherapist at the Victoria Hospital, Blackpool, and Margaret who was making her mark at Somerville College, Oxford.

With her father's gift for oratory, Margaret, (19) had helped Sqd Ldr G A Worth, in his bid for Parliament.

---

"IT'S A JOY IF IT COMES FROM JOYS"

For Summer Wear

Popular sports style frock in woollen Jersey.
Attractive pleats and tailored bodice with yoke.
Collar, belt and sleeves trimmed with contrasting material in Blue, Green and Brown.
Sizes 38 & 40

£2.8.0
11 coupons

joys

23, HIGH STREET        GRANTHAM

# Grantham in the News — 1945

## Good time mums are condemned by doctor

TOWN GP Dr Charles Frier condemned 'good-time' mums who go out on the razzle leaving their children home alone.

He said: "They leave children at a tender age regardless of their safety and welfare, sometimes with disastrous results."

He told the annual meeting of the NSPCC local branch: "The main factor was neglect to look after children by people who went off to the cinema, theatre or elsewhere.

"There are times when the inspector has had to wait with the children, sometimes for hours, until the mother decides to return home.

"The children sometimes are playing in the streets.

"The shelters make wonderful forts for them to attack but they fail to see the intervening car.

"Such danger should not be overemphasised."

NSPCC President Mrs S Greenhall said: "It is disgraceful in a Christian country there is still a need for us."

## Captured bedridden field marshal

FORMER King's School pupil Lt P Whysall, of Bottesford, bagged himself a field marshal in Germany.

The son of Grantham chemist Mr G Whysall, he was warned by a Russian slave that 96-year-old August Van Mackensen was gathering together troops for a night attack on the village.

He said: "I took a small party armed to the teeth and surround the field marshal's house.

"Imagine our surprise when we found the bedridden old general who greeted us with 'I wish you would do something about the Russian slaves stealing my poultry'.

"On the way we had picked up BBC reporter Wynford Vaughan Thomas who put it on the radio."

Van Mackersen was once dictator of Romania after Germany overran the country in 1916.

## Shell explodes in firegrate

A SHELL-given to a youngster who thought it was harmless, exploded injuring parents and their four children at Welby.

The boy had put it under the firegrate where the heat caused it to explode.

The father and his daughter (8) were detained in Grantham Hospital.

His 10-year-old son who put it there said he placed it with the ashes so it would be thrown out next day.

He did not think it was harmful.

*The American servicemen were made welcome, including these GIs at the Mid Lent Fair.*

## Thanks say the Yanks

AMERICAN servicemen with the 61 Troop Carrier Group, commanded by Col W Mitchell, gave a plaque to the people of Grantham as a token of appreciation.

The bronze plaques bore the insignia of the Army Air Corps.

The inscription read: "Sixty-first Troop Carrier Group, United States Air Forces, Barkston Heath, Lincolnshire, 1944-45.

"In appreciation of the fellowship, hospitality and understanding shown by the people and officials of the town of Grantham who far from our homes, spent many days in yours, while we were joined in destroying the tyrannical power which threatened us both."

A similar award was made by the Americans to members of the Grantham Police.

# 1945 Grantham in the News

## Coupons for kit

GRANTHAM FC needed new kit and other equipment before it could return to its soccer campaign.

After a meeting of the directors, it was pointed out that after a six year break, a fire and thefts from the pavilion left the team short of kit. An appeal was launched to ask supporters to find 430 clothing coupons.

## Denis in charge

GRANTHAM MP Denis Kendall, managing director of BMARCo, won his campaign to take over the Ministry of Aircraft Production shadow factories, on Springfield Road.

The Board of Trade overturned an earlier decision to hand the buildings to Aveling Barford.

## Never on a Sunday

GRANTHAM publicans voted against having music in pubs on Sundays by a single vote.

The Licensed Victuallers' Association chairman Mr Hart said: "The police have received objections and a Sunday music ban is the law of the land.

"The main point is that Grantham LVA wants to keep the Sabbath as quiet as possible."

## No nuptials

THE Rev T A Child left Welby after being vicar for nearly 20 years.

During that time he christened 78 villagers but was never called upon to perform a marriage ceremony.

## Grantham and Swayfield suffer brunt of bombing

OFFICIALS admitted that at one time during the war, Grantham was the most blitzed town in the UK.

There were 36 bombing raids with 155 high explosives and 400 incendiaries dropped.

Eighty-nine people were killed as a result, 83 seriously hurt and 108 slightly injured.

Eighty-three homes were destroyed due to the bombing, and 195 damaged.

The news was revealed by Sir Robert Pattinson who added that nearby Sleaford suffered no damage.

The worst hit village in Lincolnshire was Swayfield, the target of 30 high explosive bombs.

In Leicestershire, it was Bottesford which bore the brunt of the bombing, with 170 falling in one night.

Group warden Mr A E Silverwood said: "Amazingly there were no casualties."

Bottesford also gained the distinction of being the last place to be the target of a German bombing raid in England.

A lone Junker 188 made a tip-and-run raid on March 20 dropping several dud explosives and firing cannon shells.

The raid caused little damage and no casualties.

## Double inferno

TWO farms in Croxton Kerrial fell victims to stack fires within two hours.

## The heat's on referee

GRANTHAM FC kicked off their first league football match since 1940 by beating Gainsborough Trinity 5-2.

But the balmy August afternoon brought severe criticism for referee Fred Iliffe, from Peterborough.

Spectators were appalled that he played without his jacket.

**THANKSGIVING WEEK**

**WEST KESTEVEN THANKSGIVING WEEK**

NOV. 3-10

**TARGET £50,000**

SAVE FOR PEACE

# Grantham in the News          1945

## Kendall's dream car crashes

A COMPANY set up last year by town MP and BMARCo manager Denis Kendall could have brought mass-produced car-making to Grantham.

Mr Kendall aimed to win the peace with two models of a motor car which he planned to be cheap enough for every family to buy.

But his dream of a 'people's car' came to nothing after only four prototypes were built.

The photograph above was taken outside the gatehouse at Denton.

## Falling tree had policeman running for his life

A GRANTHAM policeman had to run for his life when a tree was uprooted by a tank transporter carrying a Sherman tank. It missed his head by centimetres.

Some of the branches caught the lower part of his back and legs as the tree came crashing to the ground.

An observer said: "It's the narrowest shave that any bobby will get."

The incident happened outside the Railway Tavern, St Peter's Hill.

The lime tree was flung across the pavement, some of its branches resting against the sun blind of the International Stores.

## Two by two

The six babies born after June 1 in Orston, near Bottesford, were all twins.

The Butcher boys and Spencer girls all thrived although the Miller twins failed to survive.

Mrs Spencer said: "It was a bit of a shock."

## Bishop's move

AN old boy of Grantham King's School, Dr J W C Wand, Bishop of Bath and Wells, was nominated by the King as Bishop of London, succeeding Dr Geoffrey Fisher, who was appointed Archbishop of Canterbury.

Son of a local grocer, Dr Wand was born in 1885 and after an early education at the National School, went to King's School and St Edmund Hall, Oxford, where he read theology in 1907.

## Play it for Les

LES Davey, of Dudley Road, who ran the Olympian Orchestra as a civilian, returned for his first concert in town since joining the armed services.

Mr Davey played for various Army bands and was a frequent member of bands broadcast on the radio.

## Band of hope

AN American services band played for the Girl Girls dance. British and American officers were among the guests.

CRANEMARKERS R H Neal's darts team were the first winners of the Grantham Cup as competitions were revived following the end of the war.

# 1945 Grantham in the News

*The Red Cross cadets*

## Kick out the Germans call by town councillor

A GRANTHAM councillor said German prisoners of war should not be employed on local building sites.

Replying to the Ministry of Health inquiry into the use of PoW labour, Coun G W Green said: "We do not want the streets of Grantham contaminated by anyone from Germany."

He was furious when the borough housing committee said it had no objection provided local labour was not prejudiced.

Mr Green being the only objector, the motion was passed.

Quoting Kipling, he said: "Lest we forget this is just an intimation of local softness in the matter.

"I don't think we want German prisoners in the locality.

"In fact I don't even think we want them in this country."

## Red Cross remains busy

MEMBERS of Grantham Red Cross were delighted the war was over, but it didn't mean they could take a break.

A spokesman said: "First aid is essential in peace time as well as war. We will always welcome new members."

## School a danger to children

A PETITION signed by 159 parents claimed St Anne's School was unfit for their children.

Kesteven County Council admitted that one classroom had been flooded and the floor was dangerous.

Two children were also injured by plaster falling from the ceiling.

Kesteven County Council blamed the school's managers.

Council chairman Sir Robert Pattinson said: "If the Church cannot fulfil its obligation we will have to take it over."

Coun Taylor said the school needed £1,600 for repairs caused indirectly by bombing.

He said: "The school stands on land belonging to Lord Harrowby.

"If we pull it down the land reverts to him."

## Villagers splash out

A PARTY from Hough-on-the-Hill and Brandon had that sinking feeling on a day trip to Wicksteed Park, Kettering.

Fifteen of them, including two ladies and the two bus drivers went on the boating lake.

It got to the middle, where it is three metres deep, when the boat shipped so much water, it sank, pitching them into ice-cold water.

They weren't injured.

# Grantham in the News          1946

## Mr Jones pitches in with homeless protest in a tent

BARBER Arthur Jones caused a stir when he pitched his tent in Abbey Gardens, in protest at the town's housing situation.

He said he was thrown out of his home by his landlord, who was armed with a possession order.

Mr Jones was unable to find his family alternative accommodation. He slept in the tent overnight while his expectant wife and his child stayed with friends.

Insp Curry arrived next day with workmen who took the tent down.

He spent the next two nights on the floor of his Victoria Street hairdressing salon.

Mrs Jones then stayed overnight at the Public Assistance Institution, the former workhouse, on Dysart Road.

Mr Jones said: "Since we married in 1944, we are weary of travelling the country like refugees looking for somewhere to live. I have my own business but no house.

"If there are no houses, a hut will suffice but I want a roof over my family's head."

A week later, Mr Jones, together with Flt Sgt Bennett, ex-RAF, were in the news when they squatted in Kesteven Education Committee Nissen huts on Harlaxton Road.

They chalked their names on the doors, put on padlocks and tidied up the dilapidated buildings.

Other families followed.

The town council said its waiting list for homes had reached 1,700.

## Lorry fire threat to Mid-Lent Fair

PROMPT action averted what could have been a major disaster at the Mid-Lent Fair, when a lorry caught fire near Harlaxton Road bridge.

Showmen, including a fire-eater, soon extinguished the flaming lorry owned by W B Shufflebottom, of Rotherham. Firefighters from the NFS joined them as they returned from a blaze at Fred Ayres' chip shop in Fletcher Street.

It was the first call-out for the Grantham crew since moving to a new fire station on Harlaxton Road.

## Taxi rates

NEW taxi fares agreed with the town council was 10p for up to a mile then 2.5p for every quarter-of-a-mile.

Waiting time was free for the first 10 minutes and 7.5p for each 15 minutes.

## Three new pubs planned for the town

THREE new pubs were given the green light by Grantham Brewster Sessions but three others must close and transfer their licences.

Mowbray-owned Sun Inn, Brownlow Street, was forced to transfer its licence and its name to a pub to be built on Dysart Road, opposite Heathfield Road.

Owned by the same brewery, The Three Tuns, Norton Street, was to close and be replaced by the Walton Hotel, on the junction of Harlaxton Road and Springfield Road.

Newark-based brewery Hole's Layton Arms, Grantley Street, was to shut and reappear with a similar name on Belton Lane, near Belton Avenue.

## First day trip for social club

IT was the highlight of the year for the newly-formed Ryde and Bonchurch Avenue Social Club.

For their first annual outing, the day-trippers assembled in front of the Reliance Coach before setting off for Skegness.

115

# 1946 Grantham in the News

## Absolutely pre-fabulous

A SIGNALLER blinded by a mortar bomb at Monte Cassino, Italy, and his wife, became the first tenants on the 100-bungalow prefab estate, on Belton Avenue, off Belton Lane.

Mr and Mrs C D Parker, previously of Launder Terrace, were married in December 1944.

## New Head

NINA Hewitt BA (39) of Carshalton, was appointed headmistress of the Girls' Central School, Castlegate. She succeeded Miss Jabet.

Miss Hewitt had been engaged in missionary work in southern India since 1931.

## Another new head

MR N F Bailey (40) of Barnstable, was appointed headmaster of the Boys' Central School, Sandon Road.

He succeeded Sammy Thorp who retired in July.

Mr Bailey was a radio operator during the war and played rugby union for Wasps.

## Unkindest cut

GRANTHAM hairdressers demanded canteen barbers be cut at Grantham factories.

The local branch of the National Hairdressers' Federation said Aveling Barford and Grantham Productions having their own barbers was just not on.

Spokesman Arthur Jones said: "There is no more justification for factory barbers than there is for tailors, opticians chiropodists or chemists.

## Grantham players were 'unsporting' claim

GRANTHAM Town players were accused of a lack of sportsmanship after losing the Lincolnshire Senior Cup final at Boston.

As chairman of England selectors Mr A Drewry prepared to present the victors with their trophy, the visitors slipped off to their dressing room.

The home crowd taunted the visiting supporters chanting 'where's Grantham?' and other derogatory phrases.

Mr Drewry said: "Hopefully, before Grantham FC appear in any other similar game I trust the directors will ensure that the players representing Grantham will be instructed in at least the rudiments of etiquette."

## Bed crisis at hospital

GRANTHAM Hospital was threatening to reduce the number of its beds because of a labour crisis.

Secretary John E Ray said there were 35 nursing vacancies out of an establishment of 60, caused by officialdom.

He blamed the difficulty in foreign and Commonwealth nurses getting passports and visas to come the

## Best man dies at wedding

THE best man collapsed and died at his brother's wedding.

The Rev E F Wright had just finished the service for Gertrude Cooper, of Norton Street, Grantham, and Ernest Price, of Willow Terrace, East Street, when William Price (46), of Loughborough fell backwards. He died shortly afterwards.

Guests carried him outside until a doctor confirmed he was dead.

Members of the Methodist Sunday School, Colsterworth, were out in force with their banner for this phorograph to be taken

116

# Grantham in the News — 1946

## Manor up for sale

HARLAXTON Manor was put up for sale with a £70,000 price tag.

Owner Violet Van der Elst said from her London home, she couldn't bear to go back.

She said: "Since the house was requisitioned for the war effort, trees worth £14,000 mysteriously disappeared.

"When they ploughed up 100 hectares of parkland, I felt part of me was taken away.

"It was a criminal thing to do this and there was no justification for the War Agricultural Committee to do this."

## Great gamps

AN umbrella factory became one of the first new businesses to be set up in town since the end of the war.

Owned by Kendall Ltd - nothing to do with the town MP Denis Kendall - Umbrella Ltd began with 30 women employed at the former Masonic Hall, London Road.

It planned to open a new factory employing 150 as soon as possible.

## A tailor's tall story about a pair of short trousers

A HIGH ranking officer in the Parachute Regiment was cut down to size when he ordered a new pair of trousers from High Street tailor George Mills.

The officer, one of the first to jump at Arnhem, needed a pair of trousers with a 950mm leg, selling at £1.05.

He wanted them to wear while on leave. But when Mr Mills contacted the Board of Trade he was told the maximum length for cord trousers was 820mm.

Mr Mills appealed to the Board but only received an acknowedgement for his letter. His customer returned to his unit until permission came through.

*Masons working at the top of the spire*

## On top of the world

MASONS diced with death as they rebuilt the top of St Wulfram's Church spire.

The tower and spire were wrapped in 100 tonnes of scaffolding.

Workmen had to climb the 219 steps to the top of the tower each day before starting work.

The £7,000 job meant replacing stonework at the top of the spire which had suffered serious damage from frost.

For the first time, the spire was measured accurately.

It was 86.2 metres to the tip of the weathervane.

## Youth drove a coal lorry

A 16-year-old who drove a coal lorry while under age, without a licence and uninsured walked free from Grantham magistrates court.

But his boss George Foster was fined a total of £30 for allowing it.

Both pleaded guilty.

Mr Foster admitted his regular driver had not turned up so he gave the lad permission to drive the lorry.

He said he understood, the lad was insured as he was not disqualified.

## Job losses

ABOUT 350 employees of Grantham Productions, about one-third of the workforce, were thrown out of work. It was due to the completion of a contract with the Ministry of Supply.

# 1946 Grantham in the News

## Fire station opened

A NEW fire station was opened on Harlaxton Road, by Grantham MP Denis Kendall..

It was manned by 13 full-timers and two part-time crews of 20.

## No coupons

WOMEN'S outfitters were left with hundreds of coats and dresses on their racks as customers could not get enough coupons to buy them.

Instead, mothers had to use the coupons for their growing children.

## Homes for bosses

BJORLOW Chrome and Tanners built four pre-cast concrete bungalows for senior staff on Harlaxton Road. They cost £1,200 each. Two were detached the other pair semi-detached.

## Regiment on the march

THE RAF Regiment, stationed at Alma Park during the war, moved out to a new home at Catterick at the end of the year.

The town council was given the use the former depot to house civilians.

## Names plain stupid

AT a meeting of Grantham Borough Council, Coun George Mills said roads names after councillors suggested by the housing committee should be scrapped.

He said: "We'll be ridiculed."

Ald Alfred Roberts said using their names was plain stupid. "There's no other word for it," he said.

## I've not had a bath for months says woman

A WILSFORD woman said she had not had a proper bath for months, due to the inconsistant water supply at Wilsford.

Miss Brook, representing the local WI said there were many others in the same position.

She was giving evidence at an inquiry into improving supplies to the Wilsford and Culverthorpe area.

"I have to carry water a quarter-of-a-mile uphill. It's no laughing matter.

"Children at the village school can't even have a drink of water."

Another resident said she had paid 30 visits to her pump before there was water.

She said they had to use water from a beck running through a village which was not fit for human consumption.

## Tenants refuse council offers

TEMPORARY homes being offered at former Belton RAF Regiment camp renamed Alma Park were being rejected by potemntial tenants.

The borough council took over the Nissen huts to relieve the housing shortage.

The reasons for rejection included lack of facilities for cooking, washing and heating.

## Unlucky break

GRANTHAM FC beat Lincoln City Reserves 7-1 thanks to a joiner.

The match was held up for 20 minutes while he repaired the crossbar.

With Grantham leading 4-0, Jack Macartney fired at goal and goalkeeper Parkins tipped the ball over, while hanging on to the crossbar, which snapped under his weight.

---

**JOHN H. NOAKES**
F.B.O.A., F.S.M.C.

**CONSULTING OPHTHALMIC OPTICIAN**

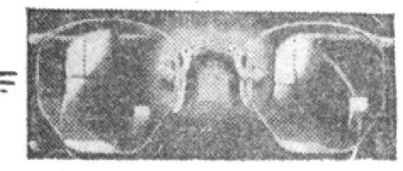

Recognised by the Ophthalmic Benefit Approved Committee for National Health Insurance Optical Benefit

13 LONDON ROAD, GRANTHAM
Telephone 648

# Grantham in the News  1946

## Burglary at the Manor

SABLE furs worth £18,000 and a safe containing £3,000 in notes, were stolen in a burglary during a blizzard at Harlaxton Manor.

Owner Violet Van der Elst was at her Kensington home, London, at the time. The theft was discovered by a nightwatchman.

It included a three-metre long Imperial Russian sable, worth £10,000.

Art treasures valued at £250,000 were untouched. Mrs Van der Elst said she had been robbed 12 times in four years, mainly at her London home.

## Shot down

TWO schoolboys were ordered to pay 91p between them after admitting using guns without licences within 17m of the highway.

They were firing at waste bins and other boys in a Dysart Road field.

*The parade passes the Horse and Jockey, High Street*

## Freedom for Yellow Bellies

THE 6th Battalion, Lincolnshire Regiment – nicknamed the Yellow Bellies - received the freedom of the borough.

This gave them the privilege of "marching through town on ceremonial occasions with bayonets fixed, colours flying and drums beating."

There was a service at St Wulfram's Church followed by a parade through town.

The honour was received by Col E J Grinling.

## Town pubs to go dry on Wednesdays

BOOZERS were forced to take a night off when the Licensed Victuallers' Association decided to shut up shop on Wednesdays.

Following an agreement with Chief Constable Weatherhogg, the new licensing hours were 8pm to 10pm for six days plus noon until 2pm at weekends.

The pubs stayed shut on Wednesdays.

LVA Secretary Charles Burch said: "We have recently had a 15 per cent cut in supplies. This is on top of cuts, so the true figure is 30 per cent.

"The public are also drinking more during the shortage."

But not all drinkers went dry.

There was an increase in platform ticket sales as drinking at the unrestricted station buffet became the Wednesday night fad.

## Plane quiet

NOISY aircraft would become a thing of the past, according the bosses at RAF Spitalgate.

RAF engineers discovered taking 150mm off each propeller considerably reduced noise levels.

It followed research following complaints from night shift workers and old people,

## Travellers keep dry

TOWN travellers were at last keeping dry while waiting for their buses.

The borough council erected three bus shelters on Dysart Road, one at the Beeden Park flat tops, one near Earlesfield estate and a third at the Earlesfield Hotel.

Three others were built opposite the hospital, near Cliffe Road and at the junction of Harrowby Lane and New Beacon Road.

Each would hold up to 30 people.

Bus stops, taken down for scrap during the war, were replaced.

# 1946 Grantham in the News

The penny-a-week committee, from left, Lionel Pinchbeck, Mrs A Hunt, Miss E M Westerhall, Mrs E Davies, Mrs F E Veasey, Herbert Hopkin, Miss M Evinson, Mrs A Dickinson, Mrs L Clements, J Tomlinson, Miss M Gregson, the Rev T J Davies, and hospital general secretary John E Ray.

## Americans buy ambulance for hospital

AN ambulance service for patients at Grantham Hospital became a reality when the American Ambulance Association of Great Britain presented the hospital with a 30hp motor.

House governor John E Ray said: "This will go far to meet a long-felt want in the district."

The service was run by a committee called the penny-a-week welfare fund committee.

They were represented by representatives of the six wards.

The Young Hospital Helpers pledged to maintain the service.

## Westgate widening would fuel homeless problem claim

A ROAD widening scheme to remove the Watergate bottleneck should be scrapped according to a county councillor.

Coun F J Cheshire said although he did not oppose the plan in principle, it was nonsense to pull down houses when there was a shortage, putting cars before people.

He said there was a housing crisis yet there were plans to knock down 30 homes with no hope of rehousing the tenants.

## Betty the beauty is crowned

THOUSANDS of people lined the streets for a parade through town of a bevy of beauties.

Later, in Wyndham Park, Betty Adams (16) was crowned Carnival Queen from 40 competitors.

Attendants were Iris Clark, of East Street, and Barbara Burden (16), of Welham Street.

Judges were GB Holiday Princess Pamela Bramah, the Hon Caroline Cust and Margaret Roberts BA.

---

**GRANTHAM & DISTRICT MOTOR CYCLE CENTRE**

Before You Buy That Motor Cycle
CONSULT

**MATT BLAND**
AGENT FOR

NORTON, HRD RAPIDE, VELOCETTE, TRIUMPH, MATCHLESS, EXCELSIOR, PANTHER, IN FACT WE CAN SUPPLY ANY MAKE OF MACHINE

Visit Our Showrooms
**LONDON ROAD, GRANTHAM**
Phone 789

REPAIRS!!!    UTMOST SATISFACTION GIVEN

# Grantham in the News  1947

## Railway station roof collapses under the weight of snow

VILLAGES isolated, schools closed, hundreds of marooned lorries, food running short, collapsed roofs ... this was the lot of Grantham people as a massive snowfall hit the area.

Forty centimetres of snow fell in just a few hours.

Drifts of up to two metres deep covered the A1 between Grantham and Stamford.

It was two days before a single lane was cleared between the two towns.

A man, woman and their young child had a lucky escape when their car was found enveloped in snow in the traffic block on Spittlegate Level.

The car was dragged out by bulldozers, its three occupants suffering from hypothermia and starvation.

Two locomotives were 'lost' at Stainby ironstone quarries. Only the tips of their funnels could be seen.

A snow plough sent to their rescue also disappeared.

A section of Grantham railway station roof caved in under the weight of snow minutes after an express had sped through.

*The roof at Grantham railway station collapsed under the weight of snow and blocked the main line*

The cast-iron pillars snapped and masses of iron, concrete and timber collapsed on to the platform and main line. No one was hurt.

A workshop roof at R H Neal's crane works, on Dysart Road, also collapsed under the weight of snow. Machinery inside was undamaged.

Conditions in the villages were the worst for many years.

Telephone cables were brought down throughout the countryside and many people had to resort to candlelight due to power failures.

## Parents in revolting mood over bomb damaged school

MANAGERS were forced to hand over St Anne's School to the county council as a controlled school, following an outcry by parents.

Parents said the school, on Dudley Road, stood a better chance of getting necessary repairs under council management.

The school, run by the Church of England, was still awaiting repairs from a bomb which had exploded nearby several years earlier.

Its heating system was very poor and water was running down the inside walls.

An inspection by education chief Dr T W G Golby revealed the condition of one ceiling was so dangerous it had to be pulled down immediately.

## Timber houses completed

THE first two of 16 Swedish-style timber houses were handed over to the rural council by contractors Rudd and Co.

They were the first of four at Barrowby with four more planned at Claypole and eight at Colsterworth.

They carried a 60 year guarantee and were let for less than £1 per week including rates.

# 1947 Grantham in the News

*The King's School band with the Lion Gates in the background*

## Memorial to Machine Gun Corps

THE King's School Combined Cadet Force band played at the unveiling of the Lion Gates memorial to the Machine Gun Corps, based there in the First World War.

The Band of the Lincolnshire Regiment also played at the ceremony.

The unveiling was performed by Lord Brownlow.

## What a right cook up!

AN RAF Regiment cook arrived at Belton Park camp as ordered only to find his entire contingent had been posted to Catterick a month earlier.

Posted from Atherinton, Warwickshire, he discovered the buildings had since been taken over by the town council for housing and renamed Alma Park.

## Food coupons are eased

BREAD units in the redesigned ration books were bigger and easier for the public to understand.

There were also more pages in them.

People were also able to register for all commodities if they wished, with the exception of milk.

The distribution centre for ration books was the Guildhall ballroom on weekdays between 9.30am and 5pm.

## Lucky escape for firemen

FIREMEN had a lucky escape when the fuel tank on an eight-wheel lorry exploded as they fought a blaze.

The lorry was carrying 14 tonnes of galvanised wire.

The driver discovered he had an overheated tyre when he stopped at the Sedgebrook cafe, on the A52. In no time his lorry was engulfed in flames.

When the firemen arrived, the fuel tank exploded.

---

### SMOKERS
Start the New Year with a New Tobacco

### BELVOIR MIXTURE
### 2/4 PER OZ.

Obtainable only from
**CHARLES LARGE**
The Tobacconist
30, St. Peter's Hill
Grantham

Phone 735

# Grantham in the News  1947

## Villagers receive stolen goods from prisoners

TEN villagers in the Colsterworth area were fined between £3.50 and £10 each for their part in receiving stolen goods from German PoWs.

The goods had been stolen from the Air Ministry store at Saltby and included madapollam cotton cloth used for covering aircraft frames, bunting and linen.

The material had been dyed and turned into blouses, pyjamas and curtains.

The prisoners had taken corrugated cladding off the hanger walls to gain access.

## Sullivan leaves Grantham

THE Grantham works of Sullivan Machinery moved from its Grange Works, London Road, to Shrewsbury after just over 10 years in the town.

The company had moved to Ruston and Hornsby's No 15 shop during the war later moving to 28 shop.

But an improving order book by the landlords meant it needed the workshops back.

A few of the workforce went to Shrewsbury but most found work with Ruston and Hornsby.

## Bus roof hits bridge

THE roof of a bus belonging to Simmons of Great Gonerby was ripped off after hitting Dysart Road main line railway bridge (pictured right).

Driver Albert Bone, of Brading Avenue, was taken to Grantham Hospital with facial injuries and a suspected broken jaw.

There were no other casualties.

A burst front offside tyre caused the vehicle to swerve across the road, hitting the corner of the bridge.

## Blue for danger

NEW mercury vapour electric lighting erected in Grantham's main street brought chaos to the railway.

LNER drivers said they were confused by the lights, especially as they crossed North Parade bridge.

The blue glow from the lights merged with the amber warning lights giving locomotive drivers the illusion of green.

Several trains were reported as passing the amber signals at high speed believing they had been given the all clear.

# 1947 Grantham in the News

## Red tape

BUILDING employers chief Mr R K Foster called for an end to red tape in the building industry.

He said it took a month to get a licence for building repairs then several weeks for permits to buy controlled materials.

## No fish - no chips

FRIED chips could no longer be bought in Grantham unless a piece of fish was bought as well, due to a national potato shortage.

The Grantham branch of the National Federation of Fish Fryers also unanimously agreed that no more than 1p worth of chips will be sold with each piece of fish.

A branch spokesman said: "This seems to be the fairest way we can make the small amount of potatoes go round."

## Died in yacht mystery

FRANCIS Fane, of Fulbeck Manor, was lost at sea, presumed dead, when the ex-Admiralty yacht Aaria blew up and sank off the Ayrshire coast.

Mr Fane (47) was joint skipper of the yacht which was being taken to Lowestoft for a refit at the time.

## Manor to be college?

KESTEVEN County Council revealed it had been interested in buying Harlaxton Manor for use as a farm institute but instead bought Caythorpe Court from the estate of the late Elma Yerburgh, a political hostess from the Victorian era, who died the previous year aged 82.

## Council protest that only two policemen were patrolling after dark

ONLY two police officers were on duty when a serious burglary was committed in the town, Grantham Borough Council was told.

Pressing for a strong protest to be sent to Lincolnshire's Chief Constable, Coun Stanley Foster said the people of Grantham deserved better protection.

The break-in, at Parker and Co's wholesale grocers and tobacconists, was only discovered the following morning.

About one million cigarettes worth more than £5,000 were stolen from the London Road warehouse.

It was believed a vehicle was parked at the rear of the premises where the 50 cartons were stored.

The thieves forced a rear gate and climbed over a dividing wall after cutting through barbed wire.

Coun Foster said local police were sent out of town nearly every day.

## She's on top of the town

COUN Mrs G A C Shipman climbed to the top of St Wulfram's Church spire, only the third woman known to have achieved the feat.

She climbed the 86.2 metres on ladders strapped to the steeple by builders repairing the fabric.

---

**FOR SKILLED EFFICIENT REMOVALS**

To anywhere within the

**BRITISH ISLES**

call or write to

**G. H. DARLEY**
(LATE A. H. IMBER)
at
**5, BARROWBY ROAD**
or
**77, WALTON GARDENS**
GRANTHAM

Part loads to London at frequent intervals      Telephone GRANTHAM 665

# Grantham in the News 1947

## Protect us from our allies plea...

TENANTS on the council-run Alma Park housing estate called for protection from Polish ex-soldiers.

The 80 Poles were employed by a contracting firm and were billeted nearby.

Residents felt so strongly they asked the Grantham British Legion for support.

A tenants' spokesman said: "We are 100 per cent against them coming." He said some women had even suggested having machine-guns and rifles to protect themselves during the day, while their husbands were away at work.

"A lot of women are alone during the day and they are strongly against having the Poles near their homes," he said.

One woman said: "Our men are away all day. It's not fair."

Town Clerk John F Guille said the Poles would live in another part of Alma Park.

"We have made all sorts of attempts to get British labour," he said. "It has not been forthcoming.

"The Polish labour is available and contractors want to use it."

**Bringing in the potato crop**

## Getting in the harvest

LADIES aided by their children were keeping the potato harvest on course. Pictured here is a gang at Long Bennington.

They were working at Mill Farm.

From left are, back – Bertha Staples, Freda Staples, Gladys Alderton and Joan Kirton; middle – Rene Elner, Edna Parnby, Sylvia Fryer and Clarice Smith. At the front are Brian and John Parnby.

## ...but they mix with the old enemy

FOLLOWING the Government's decision to grant prisoners-of-war more freedom, it was estimated that 130 Germans visited one Grantham cinema one Sunday night.

The manager said: "We have had no trouble with them yet, although the police visit from time to time."

He added that some German prisoners, especially the officers, appeared to have plenty of money and a number were accompanied by girls.

"The other evening we had three German officers escorting girls, taking the best seats at full price."

He said the Germans do not enter into conversation, even if they could speak English.

"There is a sullenness about them," he said. "If they happen to sit in the wrong seats and are asked to move they take a very dim view of it."

## Inner Street plan

A COSTLY plan leading to the demolition of the remaining houses in Inner Street was put before the Borough Council.

Councillors heard the area from Bridge End Road to St Catherine's Road including the whole of Inner Street would be bulldozed.

In its place would be light industrial units.

Under the plan, Inner Street road would remain. A new riverside highway from St Catherine's Road to Bridge End Road would be built.

# 1947 Grantham in the News

## Film magnate dies

JOHN Campbell OBE, owner of the Picture House, Central Cinema and Theatre Royal died at his home, Summer End, Barrowby Road. He was 69.

He left a son John and actress daughter Judy.

## Film stars visit

HOLLYWOOD stars Stan Laurel and Oliver Hardy visited Grantham on their way to see Stanley's 86-year-old father Arthur Jefferson at the Plough, Barkston.

The village pub was run by Stanley's sister and brother-in-law Olga and Bill Healey.

## Picking a pipe

A SHAWL parade and ornamental pipe competition were highlights of a tea party at Grantham Guildhall, for 120 'old and infirm' people of the town.

## Jobs lost

SHOP Stewards at Aveling Barford were told in January that 100 jobs at the factory would have to go.

It followed a Board of Trade decision to allocate work to Grantham Productions on Springfield Road.

## All in vane

ST Wulfram's Church weather vane, sparkling after its renovation, was returned to the top of the spire.

It was to mark the completion of major work which included rebuilding much of the spire.

## Kitchens cannot cope with school dinners

PUPILS were sent home at lunchtime on the first day of term as the demand for school dinners outweighed the ability to supply them.

At the Girls' Central School, the limit of 130 was exceeded and 50 were sent home for lunch.

Headteacher Miss Nina Hewitt said it was a hard decision to choose who should stay and who would be sent home.

She said: "Priority was given to cases of hardship and then to village children."

The central kitchens, Wharf Road, which supplied 12 schools, were at full capacity.

## Fence off our water plea

A SHAREHOLDER at a meeting of Grantham Waterworks Company demanded the supply at Stoke Lakes should be fenced off.

W. Benson, of Harrowby, said beast were allowed to drink from the water which supplies Grantham and the area.

He said: "I disagree with allowing beast to roam there and then having to clean out the tanks afterwards."

Chairman Dr G A C Shipman said: "We have in mind fencing but have received no authority to do it.

"The analysis of the water, however, has been irreproachable."

## Air cadet praised

AIR Cadet WO Peter Stevenson responded to cries for help as he cycled along Harlaxton Road, just after midnight, and found an injured airman lying on the canal towpath.

He ran to the Harlaxton Close home of Capt Grinling who called the RAF for an ambulance.

A search discovered the remains of the crashed aircraft, together with dead sheep in a field.

The bodies of both pilots of the training aircraft were also found.

Mr Stevenson was praised for his actions.

## Where's Grantham asks top Government Minister

QUESTIONS about the Grantham state-owned factory were put to Sir Stafford Cripps, President of the Board of Trade.

But when asked if he had heard about the Springfield Road factory in the town he replied: "Grantham? Where's that?"

It was explained that the factory was the one where Denis Kendall's 'People's Car' had been operating.

Sir Stafford replied: "Oh yes. I do know something about that but I cannot give any information as the matter is still under consideration at the Board of Trade."

# Grantham in the News — 1948

## Church in a spin over Sunday bikers

MORE than 2,000 people turned out at Long Bennington for a Sunday motorcycle racing programme. But it upset churchmen who complained it disturbed public worship.

The meeting was run by Newark and District Eagle Motorcycle and Light Car Club.

The club planned to stage four races a year there.

Vicar, the Rev A J Couling, said: "The most lamentable aspect of this business is that baptised people are supporting it.

"I think Christian people must endeavour to preserve the Christian society."

## Children banned from playing field

KILLJOY managers of Gonerby Hill Foot School refused a town council request to allow their playing field to be used out-of-hours.

The managers said it was too dangerous with the nearby Great North Road.

Coun Susan Brace said: "One of the factors is an ice cream depot nearby. There would be a temptation to visit it in warm weather and that would be dangerous for children."

Coun J Smith said that was a lame excuse.

He said: "The children would want ice creams whether there was a playing field or not."

*Kendall tractors being taken out for a test drive before the company was taken over by Newman Industries*

## MP's companies crash

ASSETS of Grantham Traders was a mere 71 blankets worth £50, according to a report by the official receiver.

But liabilities of the company, of which Grantham MP Denis Kendall was chairman, added up to £7,600.

A creditors meeting was told the turnover was only £3,000.

Grantham Traders was worldwide distributor for Corgi motorcycles, although for tax purposes these were funnelled through another of Mr Kendall's companies, Grantham Productions.

The latter company, based on the Springfield Road factories occupied by the Ministry of Aircraft Production during the war, went bust in 1947.

It had also produced a proto-type ill-fated 'people's car' and the Kendall tractor.

The premises were taken over by Newman Industries, a Bristol-based firm making small tractors and mining equipment.

The vacant factory next door was taken over by Ransome and Marles' Bearings, of Newark.

It created 300 jobs, half of them for women.

Grantham was a natural choice as 100 locals had been travelling to Newark every day to work for the company.

## The best sportsground in the area

A THREE-hectare sports ground, said to be the finest for 50km, was opened on Gorse Lane, in July.

The ground, for Ruston and Hornsby employees, was opened by assistant manager Lt Col H Riggall. The land was taken on a 99-year lease and had facilities for cricket, tennis, bowls, hockey and football.

A nine-hole golf course and shooting range were planned.

Run by the sports and welfare club, every employee had paid ½p weekly since 1922.

It also boasted a new pavilion built by patternmaker Harry Peel and Chris Kent with help from groundsman Mr A Shelbourne.

# 1948 Grantham in the News

## Young wives entertained

MEMBERS of St John's Young Wives Fellowship were entertained at St John's Vicarage in July, by Mrs Pelter, the vicar's wife.

The group met variously at the vicarage in Station Road and at Springfield Mission, at the bottom of Stamford Street.

**St John's Young Wives (left) Fellowship, photographed in the vicarage garden, Station Road.**

## Arthur reclaims home

ARTHUR Foster completed his own bungalow in time for his retirement

He built his Barrowby home from bricks reclaimed from air raid shelters.

A stonemason, he retired from Welby Estates in November.

## Meat prices

GRANTHAM'S fresh meat ration was cut from 4p worth of fresh and 1p of corned beef in June to 2½p of each in July.

Children's rations fell from 2p and ½p worth to 1½p of each.

No official reason was given but the cause was believed to be the London and Liverpool dock strikes.

## Town lost over season

A LOSS of £148.80 was revealed in Grantham FC's accounts.

Income from gates was £5,524 while the wage bill was £4,116.

Directors F Poole, F Steele, H Leek, J W R Carman, A E Spencer, G Pestell and W Durance were re-elected.

## Saturday night dances banned by court

ALDERMAN Bert Sindall was fuming after licensing justices banned Saturday night dancing at the Westgate Hall.

It followed a complaint of disorderly behaviour at a weekend dance. He said: "I think it was high-handed action.

"It was a complete surprise and shock to me to learn the licence on Saturdays was opposed."

Justices permitted dances Monday to Friday but strictly teetotal.

Ald Sindall, chairman of the hall's management committee, said: "The hall has been conducted quite properly and the row that happened last week was outside in the street."

Two men, who had been refused admission the previous week had begun fighting.

Chief Constable Weatherhogg said: "Police objected to the licence on account of certain complaints received, particularly with regard to Saturday nights."

The Saturday dance ban was lifted a month later although all events were strictly non-alcoholic.

## Manor from heaven

VIOLET Van der Elst sold Harlaxton Manor but refused to say for how much.

The new owner was the Jesuit Fathers who bought it to use as a Roman Catholic college.

About 200 priests moved in.

Many of the valuable French and Italian tapestries were sent to Christies of London for auction while some of the ceilings were whitewashed, covering paintings they considered 'obscene'.

---

Our Speciality - CREAM BUNS

Baker
Confectioner - Grocer

**FRANK BUSH**
(Late JUBB & SON)
92 DUDLEY ROAD
Phone 848

Quality
Service - Satisfaction
We Welcome New Registrations

WASTE PAPER SAVES DOLLARS

# Grantham in the News 1948

## Pensioners in protest over poor payments

GRANTHAM pensioners said they could hardly survive on the £2.20 per week they received from the Government.

They said prices were soaring out of control and they struggled to make ends meet.

Mrs Rawle, of Huntingtower Road, chairman of the 1,000-strong Grantham branch of the Old Age Pensioners Association, said: "I'm very disappointed with the Labour Party.

"They said if they came to power they would provide adequate pensions."

William Isaac, of Rycroft Street, said he and his wife just got by on £2.20 per week.

He said luxuries were out of the question.

*The results of the crash near North Parade*

## Missed breakfast to save lives

THE actions of a Grantham man may have prevented further collisions following a railway accident near his North Parade home.

J F Buttery heard the warning signs as he ate his breakfast. He dashed through his garden in his carpet slippers and checked the crew of a train which had run into the back of a train of iron ore wagons, were okay.

He then ran down the line to warn oncoming traffic.

Guard of the ironstone train, L F Rossington, of Newark, jumped clear seconds before the impact. His van was demolished.

An eye-witness said for several seconds wagons shot into the air, like a giant snake. No one was seriously hurt in the collision.

There was a second mishap three weeks later, when passenger coaches being shunted hit the buffers near Springfield Road.

The guards van was wrecked and guard Bob Capps was taken to hospital.

Main line traffic was not affected.

## Driver told "don't bring dying girl in here"

A DRIVER who picked up a seven-year-old girl dying from injuries received in a car accident, was turned away by householders in Great Gonerby.

Judy Goodband, of Woolsthorpe-by-Belvoir, was knocked down by a 70-year-old Letchworth doctor.

Passing motorist Edward Russell picked up the child, whom he knew was badly hurt, and seeing an open door tried to take her there. It was slammed shut as he approached.

On going to another house he was told: "Don't bring her in here. It will upset them."

He then took her to a butchers shop.

Mr Russell told an inquest he estimated the doctor was travelling at 25mph.

The child appeared to hesitate as she was two-thirds across the road and the car hit her.

## Saviour's is lost

THE final service was held at St Saviour's Church, Manners Street, before closing due to falling congregations.

Church stalwart John Cheshire said the fittings and vestments would go towards a new St Saviour's to be built in the Harrowby area.

The church had been dedicated on All Saints' Day, 1880, by Bishop Wordsworth.

# 1948 Grantham in the News

## Super Mac slams home eight goals

GOAL-machine Jack Macartney hit the target eight times as Grantham FC went on the rampage against Bradford Park Avenue Res.

Macartney slipped his minder Ron Greenwood, a future England manager, to make it both a Midland League and club individual scoring record.

But the 9-6 victory was not a record scoreline for the league as Grantham had been slammed 10-6 by Gainsborough Trinity earlier in the year.

And the story didn't finish there. At the end of the season the Avenue gained vengeance with a 6-2 victory.

## Indoor rink demand

GRANTHAM bowlers called for the town to be provided with an indoor bowling rink.

George Finn, secretary of Grantham Bowling Association, said it could be either built behind the Journal offices, on land cleared by bombs on Nursery Path, or on the car park at the bottom of Watergate.

He asked councillors to look into the matter.

He said: "It would only cost £30,000 to have an indoor rink better than the one at Boston."

## Widow goes missing in Leicester

A BOTTESFORD widow was exhausted after wandering around Leicester trying to find the coach which had taken her there.

Mrs E Clarke, of Albert Street, was with a party from Bottesford Mothers' Union, which had gone there for a diocesan MU service at the cathedral.

She was not a member of the MU but had joined the tour to see a niece. But when she returned to join the party, they were nowhere to be seen.

She said: "I had to stay the night. I was very distressed."

An MU spokesman said the bus was delayed two hours while they made an unsuccessful search for her.

## Blasted windows

MORE than 50 windows were smashed at the Girls' Central School, Castlegate, as workmen tried to blow up a disused air raid shelter in the grounds of Grantham House.

Residents in the area also reported broken windows and heavy falls of soot. The shelter was hardly damaged.

## Rent rises for council tenants

RENT increases for council tenants were announced by chairman of the town council finance committee, Alf Roberts.

Steel houses on Brittain Drive and Range Road would go up from £1 a week to £1.12.

Belton Avenue homes would go up from the same amount to £1.15 and Harrowby Lane to £1.12.

Belton Lane rents were increased to £1.23.

Coun Cheshire was against general subsidies.

He said: "It seems wrong people earning £10 to £12 a week should be subsidised by 40p a week."

## German bomb safe

A 500lb German bomb, which fell on Little Bytham in 1941, was made harmless by bomb disposal officers.

It fell into sand and shale in Mr Turner's orchard.

**HARRY HALL**
RIDING BREECHES & JODHPURS

Appointed Agents for Grantham and District

**GEORGE MILLS LTD.**
*Tailors and Outfitters*
HIGH ST., GRANTHAM   TEL. 202

# Grantham in the News　　　1948

## Airmen die in crash

AN RAF pilot and his navigator were killed when their plane exploded over Little Ponton.

Wreckage and human remains were scattered over a 100m diameter area.

Both men were based at RAF Cottesmore.

## Law hits corn men

A DECISION by magistrates that seats must be fixed in the Central cinema, High Street, caused chaos to Saturday corn markets.

Farmers wanted many of the seats moved for their weekly gathering in the same hall.

## Water on tap

WATER pipes were installed in Dawson's Alms Houses, Brook Street, at a cost of £160.

## Bidding for homes

BIDDING for terrace houses was brisk at an Escritt and Barrell auction.

Number 75 Grantley Street went for £300, 26 George Street for £440, 27 and 28 George Street for £260 the pair and 27 and 28 New Street for £230 the pair.

## Film star in town

HOLLYWOOD star Katharine Hepburn stayed at the George Hotel for a night and visited Norah Redmile's antique shop in Vine Street.

Mrs Redmile said: "I knew she was in England but I never dreamed she would come into the shop. She's awfully nice."

## Local firms win six-figure contracts to supply Poland

CRANEMAKERS makers R H Neal filled its order book with a six-figure contract to supply 60 cranes to Poland.

General manager A G Anderson said it was won in the face of stiff competition. He refused to say how much the order was worth only that it would keep the workforce busy for a year.

He said: "It will not lead to extra jobs but it will mean a guaranteed year of full-time employment for our 300 workers."

Aveling Barford also got a major order from Poland. The £100,000 deal was for 40 dumpers and 20 road rollers.

*The inventor of the Atom tractor G H F Knight (left) and the Earl of Portsmouth*

## Barford Atom explodes on scene

BARFORD (Agricultural), of Grantham, was hopeful of a big export order to Switzerland for its Atom tractor – the smallest tractor in the world.

Ideal for the narrow terraces of the Swiss countryside three were sent there for demonstration.

The machine was already proving a winner in Australia, New Zealand, Africa, the USA and Eire.

Weighing 80kg and costing only £65, the Barford Atom was also popular with the larger English garden.

It was invented by G H F Knight, of Basingstoke, whose father John Knight built the first British car.

# 1949 Grantham in the News

## Doctor and wife victims of Acid Bath Murderer

FORMER Caythorpe residents Dr Archibald and Mrs Rosalie Henderson became victims of a serial-killer.

They were among a number of victims of John George Haigh.

Their bodies were disposed of without trace by immersion into a specially prepared substance.

Dr Henderson (52) and his wife (41) both disappeared from their Fulham flat in 1948.

After killing them, Haigh, known as the Acid Bath Murderer, forged documents to gain their property worth £8,000.

He was found guilty and hanged in August.

The couple stayed in Caythorpe during the war when he was attached to the RAMC at Holy Cross, and Mrs Henderson was employed by the Air Ministry at Bridgewater House, Belton.

## Farmer caught red handed

A CLAYPOLE farmer was banned for a year and fined £10 for using red-dyed petrol.

Police checked his petrol tank after finding 45 litres of red petrol on the back seat of his broken down car.

Sgt Ledger took a sample, which revealed he was running on tax-free petrol meant for off-road vehicles only.

The farmer said one of his men must have filled the tank with the wrong petrol in error.

## Paid leave

EMPLOYEES at Aveling Barford were told they would get two weeks paid holiday for the first time.

The agreement for paid holidays was made after talks between management and shop stewards.

## House sold at auction

DOUBLE-fronted house Gorse View, Belton Lane, was sold at auction for £3,600 to Mrs Bellamy, of Foston.

## Cash hoard

COINS dating from the 18th Century were discovered during the conversion of two cottages in Church Trees, Swinegate.

## Good for you

ST Lawrence Social Club, Sedgebrook, was opened by the Archdeacon of Lincoln, the Ven Lamplugh.

Sipping a Guinness he said: "The church and pubs should work closely together."

## Major row breaks out over plans for war memorial

PLANS for a war memorial dedicated to the fallen of the Second World War were in turmoil after British Legion officials claim they were snubbed.

The town memorial fund committee, led by Mayor of Grantham George Mills, decided to wind up after the legion refused to attend their meeting.

A British Legion spokesman said: "Our President, Mr Edney, was invited as a personal guest of the Mayor, not as a spokesman.

"We consider that is a snub to us. We are opposing the memorial scheme."

The memorial fund had planned an extension to Wyndham Park, a tablet in St Wulfram's Church and an addition to the churchyard memorial.

A disappointed Mr Mills said afterwards: "I look upon it as a personal affront to myself."

## First to sign up

JOYCE Robinson (18) was the first in Grantham to sign up at the town's recruiting office for the Women's Royal Army Corps.

Joyce, of 10 Council Houses, Ancaster, was accompanied by her friend and neighbour Elizabeth Bottomley, who had already volunteered at the Lincoln office.

## Canal blaze

FIREFIGHTERS deliberately set fire to the Grantham Canal after 5,500ltrs of diesel fuel leaked from a railway tanker at the wharf sidings.

Flames and smoke leapt hundreds of metres in the air as firefighters battled to prevent the fuel getting into the boilers of a nearby factory which drew water from the canal.

## Awkward customer

BLACK and white cat Tibby, owned by Read and Son's dairy, Watergate, was discovered under floorboards after being missing for two days.

# Grantham in the News — 1949

## Queues form when sweet rationing is scrapped

CHILDREN formed queues all over town and in villages as sweet-rationing came to an end.

On Sunday, April 24, even shops which usually closed, bowed to the pressure of the new coupon-free era.

A town shopkeeper said: "One of the biggest selling lines was chewing gum, although there was a brisk trade in all kinds of confectionery.

"It became so busy at one stage, I had to call home to get extra help to serve behind the counter."

But there was one major problem. The shops had not enough stock to cope with the demand and by Monday all the shelves were empty.

**A queue forms at Cave's sweet shop on the corner of Redcross Street and Castlegate (right).**

## Waterlogged clay made rail track dangerous at speed

ONE of the biggest drainage schemes undertaken by British Railways went ahead on the East Coast line at Hougham.

For several months, King's Cross traffic was diverted at Grantham via Lincoln.

Workmen carried out reconstruction and draining the clay formation which made the track unstable.

For the previous 40 years, this part of the track had been difficult to maintain and a 40mph limit had been imposed on several occasions.

About 1,500m of piping was laid. It was discovered during the work the condition of the clay was worse than at first thought.

## Smoke supply

TOBACCONISTS said supplies of cigarettes were plentiful for the first time since the end of the war.

Even popular brands, which had been in short supply, were on display in shop windows.

But they had their fingers crossed that the forthcoming budget would not cut taxes and leave them with a surplus.

## No milk for kids

NO milk was delivered to Grantham schools as the milk shortage began to bite. Children normally had 0.2 litres of free milk every day but this was put on hold.

Co-op dairy manager, Mr S Wilson, said supplies dropped from 5,000 litres a day to only 2,300 litres in September at the Inner Street dairy.

He said he knew nothing about children being accused of selling their free milk to boost their pocket money.

Farmer Dennis Burtt, of Brandon, blamed the crisis on the weather.

He said: "It's chiefly due to the prolonged dry spell. The grass is stale and most heifers are not due to calve until October."

# 1949 Grantham in the News

## Movie star in town

FILM star David Niven arrived in Grantham to visit Nora Redmile's antique shop in Vine Street.

Mrs Redmile said: "Both Mr Niven and his wife were very charming although they didn't buy anything."

## Eddison rolls out

AVELING Barford sold its interest in road roller hire company Eddison Plant Hire to British Electric Traction.

It continued to run under its own name at Syston Lane, Belton.

## House to be a home

SUMMER End, the Barrowby Road home of Grantham cinema owner the late John A Campbell, was recommended by Kesteven County Council, to be bought as a home for the blind.

The price tag was £6,250, plus £173 surveying costs.

## Factories profitable

AVELING Barford reported a net profit of £192,107.

The plant makers paid a dividend of 10 per cent making 15 per cent on the year.

The town's other major company, Ruston and Hornsby, showed a £717,000 net profit.

## Royal horse trainer

WINSTON, the horse ridden by Princess Elizabeth at the Trooping of the Colour, was trained by Chief Insp S T Smith, of the Metropolitan Police,

He was the son of Mr and Mrs Smith, of Dysart Road.

## Pay back £15,000 MP told

GRANTHAM MP Denis Kendall was told that £15,000 he claimed he had been given must be returned.

Following a six-day High Court hearing, Mr Justice Slade ruled cash given to Mr Kendall by G M Worrall was only a loan.

The money was first presented for use in Grantham Productions and later Grantham Publications, publishers of the Grantham Guardian.

Both companies failed. Mr Slade said while Mr Kendall had not misapplied the money, he had benefited from it.

Mr Kendall said he was forced to sell his home, Brusa, on Belton Lane, to pay for the court's decision.

About 40 people were at the auction where the house, with three hectares of garden, was withdrawn at £9,750.

## A right royal upset

FIVE hundred children from Huntingtower Road School and neighbours the Springfield Secondary Modern School, were disappointed after assembling in their line-side playing field.

They were hoping to get a glimpse of Princess Elizabeth and the Duke of Edinburgh in the Royal train.

At a routine stop at the station, neither of them looked out of the window.

**LISTEN AS YOU DRIVE**
**DON'T MISS YOUR FAVOURITE PROGRAMME** — Select your
CAR RADIO SPECIALISTS
CAR RADIO HERE
**WHITE AND SENTANCE**
28. ST. PETERS HILL — RADIO — GRANTHAM

# Grantham in the News — 1949

## Bid to be youngest woman Tory MP

A GRANTHAM woman made history when she became the youngest female prospective Tory candidate.

Margaret Hilda Roberts, the 23-year-old daughter of Ald and Mrs Alfred Roberts, North Parade, was chosen to fight the Labour-held Dartford seat at the General Election.

The seat had 80,000 voters.

If victorious, she would have become one of the youngest MPs.

She said: "With vigorous campaigning we can overturn Labour's 19,000 majority."

In 1946 she was Michaelmas term president of the Oxford University Conservative Association, only the third woman to achieve the honour.

## Schoolgirl in fear of her headmistress

FEAR of her headmistress stopped a schoolgirl handing over money she found, Grantham Juvenile Court was told.

The 13-year-old said: "She is always hitting me. She prevented me from confessing I found the money."

The girl was charged with stealing 20p, the property of a school friend, but she said on oath she found only 12p on the cloakroom floor.

She pleaded not guilty.

The Girls' Central School pupil said she took the money to give to her form teacher who was engaged.

Later, when she opened her desk to take out the money, her headmistress, Miss Nina Hewitt, slapped her face and slammed the lid down on her fingers.

Magistrates dismissed the charge against the girl due to lack of evidence.

## From theft to the gallows

BREAKING open his grandmother's gas meter was the first step to the scaffold for Kenneth Strickson, of Grantham.

The 21-year-old was sent to Sherwood Borstal for the £1.42 theft, where he murdered the matron and was then hanged.

## Jail for farmer who beat girl cyclist

A FARMER accidentally knocked a 19-year-old factory worker off her bike but then attacked her with a stick, Lincoln Assizes was told.

Margaret Honora Lane was cycling home along Gorse Lane, near Keeper's Cottage, when she was overtaken by the cattle truck being driven by the Derbyshire farmer.

She was given little room and was knocked off her bike.

Appearing in court on a stretcher with serious back injuries, she said: "The lorry continued up the lane then returned.

"He stopped, stood on the running board of his lorry and asked if I was hurt.

"I said I was and he replied I should have kept on my side of the road.

"The next thing I knew, he struck me with a big stick across the eye and mouth.

"He then drove off and left me. I had never seen him before."

Pleading not guilty to assault and attempted murder, the 28-year-old farmer said he was unaware of an accident until he noticed a bicycle attached to the side of his wagon.

He told the court: "I went back to see how she was and she addressed me in an arrogant manner. She made me angry.

"My mind was very confused.

"I had no intention to harm the girl only to confuse her so she would not recognise my vehicle."

He was found guilty of grievous bodily harm with intent to murder and jailed for seven years.

# 1949 Grantham in the News

## Dog losses over £1,000

A STROXTON woman lost five top cocker spaniels worth more than £1,000 in an outbreak of hardpad which hit the Grantham area.

Mrs C Smith's top dogs had won over 100 first prizes between them.

A local veterinary surgeon said: "It has been prevalent for the past 10 years and we still know little about it. In most cases it proves fatal."

## No crest for beer

MOWBRAY'S Brewery was refused permission to incorporate the town's coat of arms on its beer bottle labels.

## Television aerial ban by council 'dictators'

COUNCIL tenants were banned from fixing TV aerials to their chimneys.

Coun William Goodliff said the town council took the decision because there was a danger from lightning strikes.

He said: "In any case, I don't think anyone likes attachments to chimneys."

He said aerials should be fixed on poles.

Ald Leonard Audus said fixing the aerials on chimneys would lead to people scrambling over roofs, causing damage to both roofs and chimneys.

Coun Tom Smith said the council was not against television sets and had no objection to aerials being fitted elsewhere on the property.

But Coun Stanley Foster accused colleagues of being "dictators."

He said: "These aerials only weight 3kg.

"We should encourage these people to go in for those modern things."

## Plough engine out of control at Croxton hill

A PLOUGH engine weighing 14 tonnes, towing a trailer with a heavy payload, ran out of control down a steep hill at Croxton Kerriel.

After overturning, it crashed through a hedge into a field and came to a standstill at the edge of a pond in the village.

The 60-year-old driver, Mr W. Crisp, remained at the controls until it overturned.

Mr Crisp said the vehicle, which usually travels at 5mph reached speeds of 40mph.

He said: "As luck would have it, no one else was on the road at the time."

Heavy dredging equipment was thrown from the trailer as the vehicle careered downhill.

Mr Crisp said: "It was all over in seconds. But I don't want another experience like that."

## Telegram boys get new motorcycles

GRANTHAM GPO's four telegraph boys were issued with motorcycles to replace their pedal power.

They took delivery of the new 125cc James machines ensuring telegrams were received even more quickly.

The lads were thrilled to bits. But it was up to them to keep them clean although they did not have to carry out their own repairs.

**Mike Matsell(right) on his new motorcycle**

# Grantham in the News — 1950

## Bench drops late night drinks charges against ex-Mayor

A POLICE raid on the Granby Inn, Market Place, early one morning during the Mid-Lent Fair, led to 40 charges, including one against a former Mayor.

Alderman B H Sindall, a butcher of 96 Westgate, was charged with consuming alcohol outside permitted hours.

The licensee faced 16 charges alleging he had supplied intoxicating liquor between 12.50am and 1.55am to eight people, including Mr Sindall.

White's wife Mary also faced 16 charges of aiding and abetting.

Seven others, all showmen from the fair, were also charged with drinking after hours.

The hearing, including a 30-minute retirement, lasted four hours before magistrates decided on the weight of evidence charges be dismissed.

## Councillors against birth control

A DECISION by Kesteven County Council to establish a birth control clinic in Grantham brought a strong reaction from one of its councillors.

Coun L. A. Webster said: "In assisting this practice, publicly we are undertaking the responsibility of obliterating a future generation."

She said the matter should be considered very carefully before spending public money.

But Ald Lilian Basford was in favour.

She said: "If people are determined to have birth control they will get it some way, but if they are not given wise, proper and perhaps professional advice, they will get it in ways which will possibly bring disaster and do a great deal of harm."

## Spare a shilling

HOUSEWIVES asked employers to put more shillings (5p) in their husbands' wage packets, to put in the gas meters.

One said: "Pennies just don't go far enough these days."

There were about 5,000 coin gas meters in the town.

*Vacu-Lug's demonstration at Great Ponton*

## Weekend and night work to complete full order books

An Anglo-American process was launched in Grantham claimed to solve the rapid wearing of tractor tyres.

The Vacu-Lug invention claimed to be the first successful method of retreading large tyres used on farm and earth-moving equipment.

The Board of Trade gave its full backing for the venture to Grantham businessman Lou Morley.

Meanwhile, Neal's Cranes, Dysart Road, built the biggest travelling crane in the country.

The £8,000 machine could move with a top load of 10 tonnes.

Aveling Barford, on Houghton Road, was also was an inventive mood, building the first British motor grader, the Aveling-Austin 99-H.

The machine which sold at £4,000 each reputedly had attracted orders worth £750,000.

137

# 1950 Grantham in the News

## Phone bill shock

A PROBE into the use of telephones by staff at the borough council was demanded by Coun Lloyd Ramsden.

He said: "The past six month's bill was £200. That's over £8 per week on phone calls.

Alderman Alfred Roberts agreed that the finance committee should investigate.

## Ladies bowled over

FOR the first time in its history, Grantham Bowling Club voted to allow lady members at their London Road greens.

It was agreed they should pay 52p annual subscription.

## Worker's Playtime

POPULAR radio variety programme, Workers' Playtime was broadcast live from RH Neal's crane factory on Dysart Road. Entertainers included Margery Manners, Kenway and Young, Leslie Adams and Tommy Kaye.

## Whisky price rise

MEMBERS of Grantham Licensed Vituallers' Association standardised the price of many spirits.

The price of whisky was set at 10p a tot and gin and rum were 9p. Brandy and wines were not part of the agreement.

## Lighting up time

WORK began on a £14,000 scheme to replace all of Grantham's gas street lamps with electric ones.

## It's a man's world for local Conservatives

LOCAL Tories were advertising for a man to replace their female agent - but they insisted they didn't want another woman.

Grantham and Sleaford Divisional Conservative Association specified they were looking for a man to take over from Mrs C G Brooks.

She had held office for the previous two years before leaving to take up an appointment in Bristol.

The local committee refused to comment on why the 'men only' decision was taken.

The proposed salary was between £600 and £800 per year depending on the applicant's experience and qualifications.

## New at St Anne's

A FORMER curate at St John's Church, Spittlegate, the Rev E E Jourdain, became the new priest-in-charge at St Anne's, Harrowby Road.

Mr Jourdain, a bachelor, took over from the Rev Edwin Millard, who retired after 40 years because of ill health.

---

**YOU ARE INVITED TO INSPECT THE LATEST**

**SUNBEAM**

At Our Showrooms

SUNBEAM 500 c.c. O.H.C. Twin, Model S7

**CAMPION DEPOT**
GUILDHALL STREET, GRANTHAM
— Telephone 114 —

# Grantham in the News — 1950

## Massive excavator overturns at Wood Hill

A GIANT 70-tonne excavator overturned while being moved from Barnestone cement works to Bescaby, near Waltham-on-the-Wolds.

It came to grief on Wood Hill, Branston, which has a one-in-seven gradient.

But even before that, the machine was in trouble.

First the transporter broke down and by the time it was repaired, it had sunk into the road and had to be jacked up.

Then as it took the bend at the summit of Wood Hill, the excavator overturned into the wood.

The road was closed for several days for the recovery operation.

**Harry Wright and the mystery cyclist**

## Who was that lady I never saw you with?

TAKEN in the Oxfordshire countryside, this is a Bristowe's Tarvia truck resurfacing a road.

On the tarbar is Harry Wright, of Grantham, who was quite oblivious to the young lady on the bicycle.

Yet amazingly, when the film was developed, he recognised her as Peggy Norton – his sister.

He did not know she was holidaying in the area at the time.

Peggy was equally unaware that her brother was working in the vicinity.

Bristowe's Tarvia was based at the Old Wharf, off Dysart Road.

## Operations cancelled as a polio precaution

TONSILS and adenoid operations at Grantham Hospital were cancelled for three weeks as a precaution, following an outbreak of poliomyelitis.

Grantham had only two victims, a five-year-old boy and a girl from Barkston. They were mild cases.

But there were five deaths at Lincoln County Hospital and a doctor working 16-hours a day battling against the disease became a victim himself.

A hospital spokesman said there was an acute shortage of nurses.

But there was also good news for the hospital.

The Sheffield Regional Board announced a £60,000 improvement package which included more than £40,000 on a new nurses' home, and improvements in pharmacy, pathology, physiotherapy and X-ray departments.

Hill View, Dysart Road, was to become a nurses training school for state enrolled assistants.

## Fast lady

LADY Ursula Manners, sister of the Duke of Rutland, stunned two pedestrians on a Grantham zebra crossing when she sped between them at 40mph.

Hairdresser Raymond Bassham and apprentice Graham Hodson both said had they not jumped out of the way, they would have been knocked down.

Lady Ursula, of The Lodge, Belvoir, told magistrates she had "no recollection of any unusual occurrence at all".

Magistrates fined her £5 with 88p costs.

# 1950 Grantham in the News

## Len's a big hit

YORKSHIRE and England batsman Len Hutton gave a film lecture to 600 people at the Springfield Road social hall.

He was guest speaker for Grantham Cricket Club.

In the afternoon he had tea with fellow Yorkshiremen Mr and Mrs Frank Parker at their North Parade home.

## Denis is defeated

Denis Kendall, Grantham MP, for the past eight years, was beaten by Tory Eric Martin Smith at the General Election.

He came third polling 12,792 votes with Labour's A E Millet second.

## Indoor market

A PLAN to take Grantham market off the streets and build and indoor one was recommended by the council's general purposes committee.

## New village hall

SWAYFIELD village hall was opened by Cmdr E. Tom Clegg.

The 160 villagers raised the £250 required to build it.

## Margaret second best

MARGARET Roberts, daughter of Alderman and Mrs Alfred Roberts, North Parade, failed to win Labour stronghold Dartford for the Conservatives at the general election.

Miss Roberts was second with 24,490 votes to Labour's 38,128 in a three-cornered fight.

## Children of neglectful mother had one ragged frock each

A MOTHER was jailed for three month's for child neglect, after magistrates heard her two children had only one frock each.

Her two daughters aged five and two were taken into care by the NSPCC.

The condition of the children had been reported by GP Dr Peter Maxted who saw them playing on a wet floor in a dirty bedroom.

He said they were completely naked, with verminous heads and bodies.

A neighbour in Tennyson Avenue said they had only one frock each, which were torn down the back.

They wore no underwear and their hair was matted.

The neighbour said she often saw the little girls standing naked on the window sill.

Both the 24-year-old mother and her estranged husband pleaded not guilty.

The father, who told the court he sent his wife £1.50 a week, was fined £5 for leaving the children to his wife's mercy.

Sentencing the woman to three months in jail, Magistrate Rothwell Lee said: "It is amazing there are such creatures as you living in this civilised country."

The children were put into the care of the local authority while the father was ordered to pay 50p weekly towards their upkeep.

## Boys had suffered enough

TWO young boys were discharged of stealing potatoes after Grantham Magistrates ruled they had been punished enough.

Chairman Stanley Foster was told both had been thrashed by their respective fathers and then caned by their headmaster.

He congratulated the parents involved for their action.

## Broken fall

WINDOW cleaner Derek Meek had a lucky escape when he fell 10 metres.

He was working at the rear of the Talbot Cafe, Market Place, when he slipped from a window sill. His fall was broken by an outhouse roof.

## Rats! We are sunk!

AN Aveling Barford diesel roller became fast in Sydney Street - because of rats.

The roller driven by Mr W Harris, of Harrowby Lane, was travelling over a freshly patched piece of road when it gave way.

Rodents boring their way through towards the sewers caused the subsidence which trapped the 12-tonne roller.

It was later freed by using a mobile crane.

# Grantham in the News          1950

## New laws threaten milkmen's livlihoods

NEW regulations banning the sale of milk from churns threatened the livelihood of most local retailers.

The new law stopped milk being poured from one container to another in the street.

In future, all milk had to be bottled and even cardboard bottle tops were stopped.

All bottles had to be sealed with a metal cap.

**Mr Simpson (right) with the milk churns which were soon to be outlawed**

## Scouts are heroes at cottages blaze

THE roofs of a block of four thatched cottages at Woolsthorpe-by-Belvoir, were destroyed in an Easter Monday fire, made more fierce by high winds.

And it could have been worse had it not been for the intervention of a group of Grantham boy scouts camping in nearby Belvoir Park.

They helped villagers remove furniture and personal belongings from the homes.

Firefighters from Grantham, Melton and Loughborough fought the blaze.

The furniture was stored in the Belvoir Hunt's stables.

One of the occupants, Mrs Saddington, said they were just finishing their meals when the fire broke out.

She said: "The scouts and the people of the village were champion.

"The scouts formed a chain bucket system and water was used from the soft water tubs, cisterns and the nearby lake."

The 2nd Grantham and Harlaxton troops were joined by the 7th Grantham Troop and the lads from Woolsthorpe.

The cause of the blaze was a mystery.

### Help with uniform

A GRANTHAM girl who passed for the 11-plus for Kesteven and Grantham Girls' School nearly missed out because her parents couldn't afford to pay for her uniform.

But following the intervention by the Grantham branch of the British Legion, the Education Minister lifted his ban on grants.

Town MP Eric Martin Smith, who took up her case, said the girl would have sacrificed her academic future without the Minister's change of heart.

## Market trader fined for nylon overcharge

A MARKET trader was fined a total of £40 by Grantham magistrates for selling nylons in the town market for more than the permitted price.

A woman Board of Trade inspector asked the vendor how much his nylons were and he told her they were 59p per pair.

She told the court that the maximum price allowed for nylons, which were not fully fashioned, was 46p per pair.

Magistrates said that it was a disgrace that women were being asked to pay outrageous prices at times of austerity.

They fined him £25 for the offence and a further £10 for failing to produce an invoice.

Magistrates also ordered him to pay a further £5 towards prosecution costs.

# 1950 Grantham in the News

## Thirty-six in hospital following bus crash

FIVE ambulances ran a shuttle service to Grantham Hospital after a bus crashed and overturned at Burton Coggles.

Passengers were returning from a darts evening at the Woodhouse Arms, Corby Glen, when it overturned into a cornfield.

Villagers and a woman doctor were first on the scene, rescuing trapped passengers and rendering first aid.

The 36 passengers were taken to Grantham for treatment. Some were badly hurt and others were suffering shock and cuts from flying glass.

Owner Ron Foster, of Grantham, said: "It was a new bus which I have had only three weeks. It was due to go to the White City Stadium tomorrow, taking a party of boxing enthusiasts to see the Lee Savold versus Bruce Woodcock World Championship fight."

An examination by the Ministry of Transport found no mechanical defects.

## Lights go out like magic in conjuring show

A PARTY for estate workers came to an abrupt halt when a building which housed a generator caught fire at Culverthorpe Hall.

It was discovered as the lights went out as a conjuror was practising his magic.

Three fire crews from Grantham, two from Sleaford and one from Bourne attended the blaze.

At its height the blaze in the two storey-building was threatening to spread to estate workers' cottages.

The generator, oil engine and compressor, which supplied power to the estate were destroyed.

The hall was never in danger, although was left without lighting and heating.

Villagers and shopkeepers responded to an SOS by owner Col Bowlby lending him oil lamps and heater until the plant was replaced.

## Memorial to civilian war dead

MAYOR of Grantham Ald William Dale, unveiled a memorial to Grantham's civilian war dead in Grantham cemetery.

Of the 85 civilian air raid victims of the Second World War, 69 were buried in the cemetery. One body was never recovered.

The 8m high memorial had a miniature garden with dwarf roses.

It included the names of 20 people who were buried in a communal grave.

Forty-nine were buried privately and 15 were interred in their own parishes.

---

## Television aerials

The best results are not always obtained from the most expensive television aerials.

When chosing the type of aerial to be used, field strength and signal-to-noise ratio at the site should be taken into careful consideration.

Just on reason why you should consult specialists in television.

### BURGESS & COULSON
RADIO AND TELEVISION ENGINEERS
24 High Street, Grantham

-Tel. 395 -

# Vicars and Rectors of St Wulfram's Church from 1223

Until 1714, there were two incumbents, the Vicar of Grantham North and the Vicar of Grantham South

## Vicars of Grantham South

1225 Richard of Newerk
1234 Will of Ferneden
1245 Thomas
1263 Michael of Lincoln
1277 John of Hennington
       John of Neots
1302 Walter ?
1303 Robert de Stakethern
1335 Robert de Wilyen
1352 John of Kelby
1377 Richard of Frieston
1382 William of Sibthorpe
1397 William of Billynburg
1414 Henry of Skyndelby
14.. Richard Wytham
1474 Thomas Dalby
1476 Edmund Coynson
1478 Thomas Isham
1500 William Marshall
1501 Richard Day
1506 Roger Thurley
1515 John Edmund
1516 Richard Sheppard
1545 William Rede
1552 Thomas ffuller
1559 John Only
1560 Richard Smythe
1561 Stephen Knighte
1563 Jasper Turnbull
1581 Humphrey Travers
1586 Robert Bryan
1601 Nicholas Walker
1607 Thomas Deane
1625 Peter Tyley
1633 Roland Greenwood
1634 Edward Harryes
1639 Edward Dixe
1670 Samuel Burnet
1711 John Harrison

## Vicars of Grantham North

1223 Bononius
1231 John de Colsterworth
1264 Robert de Hinton
1284 William de Hackburn
1291 Henry de Witteneshale
1294 Robert de Thorp
1307 William de Ayleston
1316 Thomas Moysant of Croxton
1317 Richard Blound
13.. John ?
1335 Henry de Pirie
1345 Thomas of Chelry
1349 Geoffrey de Willan
1376 John Wright of Yerdeburgh
1383 Will of Dorlee
1384 Hugh de Dorlee
1407 John Appulton
1423 John Day of Berowe
1431 John de Hylle
1454 William Barneswell
1459 Richard Dawes
1486 William Spenser
1511 John Elton
1519 William Pickenham
1519 John Dent
1535 John Wilkinson
1548 John Clarke
1552 Oliver Heywood
1554 William Harberd
1557 Richard Smith
1563 John Clarke
1574 Francis Bannister
1580 Humphrey Travers
1586 Robert Bryan
1597 Stephen Lodington
1608 Thomas Dilworth
1646 Thomas Redman
1653 ? Seabrooke
1655 ? Harrison
1656 Humphrey Babbington
1662 Henry Johnson
1666 John Hanson
1701 Samuel Burnet

## Vicars of Grantham

1714 John Harrison
1736 Richard Easton
1786 George Barington
1792 Thomas Easton
1817 William Potchett
1856 George Maddison
1874 Jacob Clements
1879 Cecil Edward Fisher
1883 William Glaister
**1905 Welbore MacCarthy**
1910 Wm Isaac Carr-Smith
1917 Bernard Walter Hancock
1928 Algernon Augustus Markham
1939 Harold Leeke
1958 Graham Sansbury
1977 Rex Howe
1986 Bob Reiss
1996 Christopher Andrews

143

Grantham in the News 1851-1875
ISBN 1-902950 02 X

Grantham in the News 1876-1900
OISBN 1-902950 04 06

The Changing Face of Grantham
ISBN 1 85983 431 0

*Other books about Grantham by the same author*

For details visit: GranthamPast.com

Grantham in Focus Vol 1
ISBN 978-1-84547-142-2

Grantham in the News 1951-1975
ISBN 978-1-84547-141-5

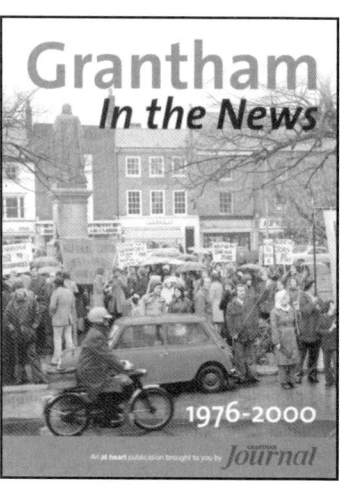

Grantham in the News 1976-2000
ISBN 978-1-84547-173-6

Grantham in Focus Vol 2
ISBN 978-1-84547-209-2